Date of the Last Supper

THE DATE OF
THE LAST SUPPER

ANNIE JAUBERT

ALBA HOUSE
a division of St. Paul Publications
Staten Island, N.Y.

Translated by Isaac Rafferty

Original Title:

    La Date de la Cène. Calendrier biblique et liturgie chrétienne (*Gabalda*).

Nihil obstat:

    Donald A. Panella, S.T.L., S.S.L., M.A.

        Censor Deputatus

Imprimatur:

    ✠ Franicis Cardinal Spellman

      Archbishop of New York

March 23, 1965

Library of Congress Catalog Number 65-17975

Designed, printed and bound in the U.S.A. by the Pauline Fathers and Brothers of the Society of St. Paul at Staten Island, New York as part of their communications apostolate.

Contents

ABBREVIATIONS

A. J.	*Jewish Antiquities*
B. J.	*The Jewish War*
C D C	*Sadocite Document* or *Writing of Damascus.*
C. S. E. L.	*Corpus Scriptorum Ecclesiasticorum Latinorum,* Vienna.
D. A. C.L .	*Dictionnaire d'Archélogie chrétienne et de Liturgie,* Paris.
D. B. S.	*Dictionnaire de la Bible, Supplément,* Paris.
D J D	*Discoveries in the Judaean Desert, I, Qumran Cave I,* Barthélémy - Milik, Oxford, 1955.
G. C. S.	*Griechische Christliche Schriftsteller,* Leipzig.
H. U. C. A.	*Hebrew Union College Annual,* Cincinnati.

J. B. L.	*Journal of Biblical Literature*, Philadelphia.
J. Q. R.	*Jewish Quarterly Review*, Philadelphia.
J. T. S.	*Journal of Theological Studies*, Oxford.
P. G.	*Patrologia graeca*, Migne, Paris.
P. L.	*Patrologia latina*, Migne, Paris.
P. O.	*Patrologie orientale*, Graffin - Nau, Paris.
Q	Qumran
1 Q - 4 Q	Cave 1 - Cave 4 of Qumran.
1 Q M	*Book of the War.*
1 Q S	*Manual of Discipline* or *Rule of the Community.*
1 Q Sa	*Rule of the Congregation.*
R. B.	*Revue biblique*, Paris.
R. E. J.	*Revue des Etudes juives*, Paris.
R. H. E.	*Revue d'Histoire ecclésiastique*, Louvain.
R. H.R.	*Revue d'Histoire des Religions*, Paris.
R. S. R.	*Recherches des Sciences Religieuses*, Paris.
Str. - Bill.	*Kommentar zum Neuen Testament aus Talmud und Midrasch*, Strack - Billerbeck, Munich.
T. M.	Massoretic text.
T. U.	*Texte und Untersuchungen*, Leipzig.
Vig. Christ.	*Vigiliae Christianae*, Amsterdam.
V. T.	*Vetus Testamentum*, Leyde.

FOREWORD

THE date of the Last Supper is linked with the problem of the day of Jesus' death, a question which has occupied exegetes since the end of the second century. In the present work a new solution is proposed, based on an ancient Jewish calendar, recently discovered, and on an Eastern patristic tradition which has all at once been illumined by the new calendar.

The plan of the present study is determined by the shape of the problem. The first task is to assemble the elements from which the ancient calendar may be reconstructed, to investigate its origins and history, and then to trace its subsequent, important influence on the Christian liturgy. This is the essential basis for establishing the fact that it was in a liturgical context that there grew up a Christian tradition placing the Last Supper on Tuesday evening. This tradition itself next occupies our attention: its extent, the conditions in which it originated, possible explanations for it. Only in the final section will the Gospel documents be taken into consideration in order to establish to what extent the new hypothesis respects the internal requirements of the text, satisfies their demands and increases their intelligibility and coherence.

Evidently, an enquiry such as this calls for disscussion of matters pertaining to very many fields: from the Old Testament to the New Testament and to patrology, from ancient Judaism to rabbinical Judaism, to say nothing of calendar systems or of the broad area of ancient Oriental languages. For these reasons this small volume is intended primarily as an invitation to research. The problems raised are so numerous, sometimes so essential to the argument, that each specialist must test the solidity of the hypothesis in so far as it enters his own field, and it is for him to propose solutions to the new question-marks raised at each step of the present study. In order to facilitate this task it seemed useful to assemble here the information already contained in three articles,[1] adding certain new facts and new interpretations. Developments of particular points which would have obscured the issue or interrupted the flow of the argument have been relegated to the appendices.

This work owes a great deal to the sympathy and encouragement of several specialists. I am more than a little embarrassed that I cannot name them all. It may, however, be permissible for me to offer my thanks to Mr. H. Ch. Puech, professor at the Collège de France, and to express my gratitude to Mr. H. I. Marrou, professor at the Sorbonne, without whom these investigations would never have been undertaken.

First Part

An Ancient Jewish Calendar

CHAPTER I

THE CALENDAR OF *JUBILEES*

THE principal document which has made possible the rediscovery of an ancient Jewish calendar is the *Book of Jubilees*.[1] One of the apocrypha, antecedent to the Christian era, this work takes up the traditions contained in the biblical *Book of Genesis,* developing, adapting and transforming them in accordance with the interests of the environment of its origin. By both reason of its extent and of the variety of subjects of which it treats, it is an extremely valuable work for us. This new edition of *Genesis* is nothing less than a *Summa* which fuses together various traditions, fragments of epic literature, liturgical extracts, hagiographical writings, the whole being unified by a strict chronology which gives form to the book and is based on the weeks of the year and on the jubilees. It is difficult to date this collection; but if by date one understands the period in which the work was drawn up in its present form, then it would seem reasonable to suggest the last decades of the second century, B.C. (Appendix I)

This book has attracted attention by reason of its easily discernible internal affinities with the documents of the sect of Qumran. However, a close study of *Jubilees* was of itself sufficient to discover a key to the interpretation of the calendar which it follows. It was, nevertheless, the impetus of the recent discoveries which stimulated research and comparisons. From the very beginning of these finds fragments of the *Book of Jubilees* were brought to light. Since then, the number of manuscripts found has grown considerably,[2] an indication of the obvious importance enjoyed by *Jubilees* in the sect. But well before the discoveries of the desert of Juda, a document which is now seen to be related to the group of Qumran, the *Writing of Damascus*, proclaimed that whoever desired to return to the Law of Moses and to submit to its prescriptions must observe the "book of the division of time" (*CDC* XVI 1-5). In tones similar to those of the *Book of Jubilees* it declared that the whole of Israel had fallen into blindness; the members of the sect alone defended the authentic calendar. To those alone who had kept his commandments had God revealed his sacred sabbaths and his glorious festival days (*CDC* III 13-15). The sabbath-day should be kept according to its strict observance, the festival days and the days of fasting according to the reckoning of the members of the New Alliance in the territory of Damascus (*CDC* VI 18-19). In its turn, the *Rule of the Community* laid it down that dates should not be anticipated nor festival-days postponed (*IQS* I 15-16), and set out a division of time remarkably close to that of *Jubilees* (*IQS* X 5-7). The very recent discovery of a fragmentary liturgical calendar on the site of Cave 4Q identifies definitively the calendar of *Jubilees* and that of the sect.[3]

The texts just cited already introduce us to an ancient mentality for which time is sacred.[4] Days are sacred because God has prescribed them in the Law of Moses and thus they form part of the commandments of the Alliance; such is the teaching of the sect. Days are sacred because whoever enters into conflict with the calendar places himself in contradiction to the harmony of the heavens, to the courses of the stars ruled by angels, to the heavenly assemblies who also observe the festival-days of a liturgy common to angels and men; such is the concept which emerges from the *Book of Jubilees* and from its close relation, the *Book of the Luminaries of Henoch*.

For why have so many Israelites perished and fallen captive to foreign peoples?

"Because they have forgotten my commandments and the festival-days of my alliance, and my sabbaths" (Jub., 1,10; cf. Jub., 1,14).

Why are there these fratricidal disputes between the members of the holy people?

"Because they have forgotten commandments, alliance, festival-days, months, sabbaths, jubilees..." (Jub., 23,19).

17

Since the creation and its seventh day, God keeps the sabbath in heaven with the highest angels (Jub., 2,17-18). From the day of creation to the days of Noah, the festival of Weeks has been celebrated in heaven (Jub., 6,18). The revolutions of the stars which preside over the calendar proceed in an awesome rhythm "in accord with the number of the angels, and they keep trust with one another."[5]

It may thus be understood why the venerable Henoch, who

"learned the scriptures, knowledge and wisdom, has written in a book the heavenly signs (of the zodiac) according to the order of their months, in order to make known to men the days of the year, the ordinance of the months and the sabbaths of the years" (Jub., 4,17-18).

Happy are those just men whom Henoch has initiated into the secrets of the heavens,

"happy are those who walk in the way of justice and who do not sin as do those who are sinners in the calculation of all their days" (I Hen., 82,4);

happy are those who "give ear to learn this widom" (I Hen., 82,3), this wisdom which the Lord has written for ever on the tables of the heavens.[6]

Henoch had entrusted these revelations on the secrets of the heavens — together with other precepts — to his son, Methuselah; Methuselah had handed them on to Lamech, Lamech to Noah, and Noah to his sons (Jub., 7,38-39). Through Sem, Abraham and Jacob the traditions were handed down as far as Levi, the great treasurer of the secrets of the Fathers.[7] Jacob had given

> "all his books and all the books of his fathers to Levi, his son, that he might preserve them and renew them (by copying) for his children down to the present day" (Jub., 45,16).

At the end of the chain of transmission, accordingly, there is *Levi*. Thus, on the the evidence of *Jubilees* itself, the traditions of the Fathers had been preserved in a priestly environment. Moreover, all evidence confirms the priestly character of the context of *Jubilees* and of the Qumran sect.

What, then, is the character of the *sacred calendar* so sternly defended by the *Book of Jubilees* in opposition to the mass of the people of Israel who have gone astray in imitation of the Gentiles? It will be recalled that the Jewish calendar, still in use today, and which, since it was followed by the Jewish authorities in the first century of our era, we shall call the *official* or legal calendar, is based on twelve lunar months of 29 or 30 days (the lunar month having 29 days, 12 hours, 44 minutes). These lunar months are given their Babylonian names: Nisan, Iyar, Sivan, and so on. Twelve lunar months, composed alternately of 29 or 30 days, form a total of 354 days, so that there is a shortage of 11¼ days with respect to the solar year. To bridge this gap a supplementary month was added every two or three years to the last month of the year. This is quite different from the calendar taught to Moses by the angel in *Jubilees*:

> "Command the children of Israel to observe the years according to this reckoning—364 days. These days will

constitute a full year. They are not to disturb its days and festivals....If they do not observe His commandment, they will disturb all their seasons and the years will be out of place....And all the children of Israel shall forget, and they shall not find again, the way of the years, and they shall forget the new moons and the seasons and the sabbaths, and they shall be deceived in the ordering of the years....The division of days is laid down on the tablets of the heavens, lest they forget the festivals of the alliance and walk according to the festivals of the Gentiles, following their errors and their ignorance. For there are those who shall base their observations on the moon — even though it disorders the seasons and arrives from year to year ten days too soon. They shall make of a detestable day a day of witness, of an impure day a day of festival, and they shall confuse all the days, the holy with the impure and the impure with the holy; for they shall be deceived on the months, the sabbaths, the festivals and the jubilees....After your death they shall no longer make a year of only 364 days and for this reason they shall be in error regarding the new moons, the seasons, the sabbaths and the festivals and they shall partake of every species of blood" (Jub., 6,32-38).

This forthright text is already clear in itself. But it must be complemented by the passage immediately preceding it (Jub., 6,23-30). The year must contain 364 days *only*, exactly 52 weeks which compose the *complete* year (Jub., 6,30). The year is divided into four seasons, each of thirteen weeks; and the first days of each season are days of remembrance (Jub., 6,23-29). There is no doubt—and this view will be confirmed by what follows—that this reckoning of 364 days, exactly divisible by seven, is intended to bring into prominence the days of the week. It means that the liturgical festivals will fall from year to year *on the same day of the week*. This is an essential characteristic of this calendar. In addition, the months are of 30 days (Jub., 5,27) and the year contains twelve months (Jub., 25,16). In contrast to the official calendar, these months are always named by their *number*. Every three months an intercalary day must be added in order to obtain the 91 days or 13 weeks which form the season (91 X 4=364 days). The same distribution of days is found in the related book, the *Luminaries* of Henoch.[8]

The figure of 364 days is evidently the figure divisible by seven nearest to the solar year. For this reason we may describe the calendar of *Jubilees* as a solar calendar. It is precisely the intention of its author to rely on the sun, and not on the moon which arrives "every year ten days too soon" (the difference between 364 and 354). Yet even though the difference from the true solar year is much less important in the calendar of *Jubilees* than in the official calendar, it still exists and consists in $1\frac{1}{4}$ days each year. At the end of a jubilee—49 years—the gap to be bridged would be $61\frac{1}{4}$ days. Now such a discrepancy is impossible in the system of *Jubilees* which takes account of the "heavenly signs" (Jub., 4,17-18; I Hen., 72,13-19), and hence of the solstices and equinoxes, and whose liturgical festivals are correlated with the seasons of the year—for example, the festival of offering the first sheaf of corn, or that of the first fruits of the harvest (the festival of Weeks). As regards the intercalations in this calendar we are reduced to conjecture. The difficulty has not yet been solved.[9]

There is, however, another problem, equally difficult, which, until recent years, had to be faced by the student of the *Jubilees* calendar. This is the question of *the date of the festival of Weeks*. This Feast of Weeks, which later came to be known by the Greek name of Pentecost (Tob., 2,1), is also called in the Pentateuch the Harvest or First-fruits Festival.[10] It holds an important place in the *Book of Jubilees*, for it is the festival of the annual renewal of the alliance (Jub., 6,17) and it is an easy matter to identify it with that of the sectaries of Qumran (*IQS* I 16-11 21). Now this capitally important festival must fall — this is one of the strictest points in the *Book of Jubilees* — in the middle of the third month (Jub., 15,1; 16,12-13), that is, on 15 of month III.[11] How is this requirement of *Jubilees* to be reconciled with the rule of *Leviticus* that the Feast of Weeks occurs fifty days after the offering of the first sheaf which is weighed on "the day after the sabbath" (Lev., 23,15-16; cf. Deut., 16,9)?

According to the official Jewish calendar, the "sabbath" referred to is the first day of unleavened bread, which was a day of rest. Consequently, according to the legal calendar, the fifty days are counted from 16 Nisan (Nisan, 30 days; Iyar, 29 days) and the Feast of Weeks is celebrated on 6 Sivan, a date which may fall on any day of the week. Now, if the same principles were applied to the *Book of Jubilees*, starting from 16 of month I (months I and II having each 30 days), the Feast of Weeks would fall on 5/III, which is in contradiction to the rule expressly formulated by *Jubilees*. In order that the Feast of Weeks take place on 15/III it is necessary that "the day following the sabbath" fall on 26/I. But how is this possible?

This "day following the sabbath" has, indeed, always been the object of lively controversy. Its echo is already heard in the Mishna and the Talmud which voice opposition to the Boethusians who interpreted "sabbath" literally as the seventh day of the week and for whom, consequently, Pentecost always fell on a Sunday (*Menahot* 10,3; cf. Hagiga 2,4). It is of interest to notice that these Boethusians of the Talmud are "Sadducees"—whatever these sons of Sadoc are, they belong to a priestly background. But it is also important to notice that they must have represented an extremely ancient tradition since the Samaritans—whose priestly connections are certain—still celebrate Pentecost on a Sunday and since this opinion is shared by the Karaite Jews.[12]

There has been no lack of critics who have interpreted the "day following the sabbath" of Lev., 23,15, as the first day of the week (Sunday).[13] If this hypothesis had been pursued, applying it to the *Book of Jubilees*,[14] (taking into account the priestly origin of the latter, and given the fixity of the liturgical festivals in this calendar) the days of the week on which all the other liturgical feasts fell would long since have been discovered. However, another factor embarrassed investigators, for to admit a day following the sabbath on 26/I, and thus to admit a Saturday on 25/I, was to make the month begin on Wednesday, 1/I. Yet it appeared altogether absurd to have the beginning of the year on a Wednesday (the fourth day of the week) and not on a Sunday (the first day). As a result, the requirements of *Jubilees* were lightly set aside as belonging to the realm of fantasy.

23

The contribution of Fr. Barthelemy has brought the question a decisive step forward. He has adduced a note of the Arab writer, Al-Biruni, who, in his *Chronology of Oriental nations,* speaks of a sect of the Magarya or "people of the cave" (their books having been found in a cave). Now these Magarya offer several resemblances to the sectaries of Qumran: [15]

"Abu-Isa Alwarrak speaks in his *Kitab al-Makalat* of a Jewish sect known as the Maghariba,[16] who claim that festivals are legal only when the moon appears full in Palestine *in the night of Wednesday which follows the day of Tuesday,* after sun-set. This is their New Year's Day. It is from this day that the days and the months are reckoned and that the annual cycle of festivals begins. For God created the two great givers of light on a Wednesday. Likewise, they do not allow that the *Pasch* fall on any day other than *Wednesday*. However, they consider the obligations and rituals prescribed for the Pasch as necessary only for those who live in the land of Israel. All of this is opposed to the customs of the majority of the Jews and to the prescriptions of the Torah."[17]

We may leave aside for the moment the lunar question to which a special appendix is dedicated. The justification for beginning the year on the fourth day of the week (Wednesday) is the fact that *the stars were created on the fourth day*. For it is precisely from the moment when the stars began to regulate the course of time that the days, the months and the cycle of festivals began to run. If, then, the year is made to begin on a Wednesday in *Jubilees,* the Pasch (15/I) also falls on a Wednesday, as the text states, and 26/I is then, indeed, a Saturday. But the calculation of fifty days must be taken from the Saturday *which follows* the octave of the Pasch and not, as is the practice of the Samaritans and Karaites, from the Saturday within the octave. Here lies the solution to what was up to the present one of the most obscure points concerning the calendar of *Jubilees*.

Another approach, independent of the date of the Feast of Weeks, and of all external criteria, clearly confirms the fact that the year begins on Wednesday in *Jubilees*. For, apart from indications, as yet extremely obscure, of weeks of the year and of jubilees, the *Book of Jubilees* has scattered throughout its length and punctuating the history of origins and the story of the patriarchs, a series of dates, expressing numerically the days and the months. The patriarchs undertake many journeys, both in *Genesis* and in *Jubilees*. What is of interest to us is the fact that the author never permits the patriarchs, model Israelites as they were, to travel on the sabbath day, in conformity with the law laid down in Jub., 50,12. Our task, then, is to assemble all *the days of travel* dated by the author and to draw up the corresponding table of days of the week according to the reckoning characteristic of *Jubilees*. We shall begin with the journeys of Abraham.

Jubilees	*Travel days*	
16,11	Abraham sets out in the middle of month V. The "middle," by analogy with the Feast of Weeks, is 15 of the month.	15/V
17,15	Mastmah demands the sacrifice of Isaac on 12 of month I.	12/I

18,1-17	Abraham, in obedience to the command of God, rises early in the morning, thus on 13, comes to Mt. Sion on the third day, thus on 15.[18]	13/I 14/I 15/I
	He sets out again the same day for Bersabee; thus the same length of time for the return journey, two days (16 and 17 of month I)	16/I 17/I
27,19	Jacob arrives at Bethel in the evening of 1 of month I	1/I
29,5	Jacob sets out for Gilead on 21 of month I	21/I
	Laban reaches Jacob on 13 of month III	13/III
29,6-7	*Certain halt on 14 of month III.*	
29,13	Jaboq passed on 11 of month IX	11/IX
31,3	Going up to Bethel on 1 of month VII	1/VII
33,1	Jacob's visit to Isaac on 1 of month X	1/X
34,12	Sending of Joseph's garment on 10 of month VII	10/VII
44,1	Jacob's departure on 1 of month III	1/III
44,8	Departure from the Well of the Oath on 16 of month III	16/III
45,1	Arrival in Egypt on 1 of month IV	1/IV

In the table which may be drawn up from these dates, the days of the week are set out vertically, each indicated by a letter of the alphabet, and the days of the months, indicated by ordinal numbers, are set out horizontally. Since the year is composed of four trimesters, each equal to 13 weeks and with three months of 30 days plus an intercalary day, the disposition of the days of the week in each trimester is symetrical. Because of this correspond-

26

ence, it is sufficient to set out one trimester, its disposition being valid for the other three. In this basic trimestral table, the first month stands for the first month of each trimester —that is, for the first, fourth, seventh and tenth month of the year; the second month stands for the second month of each trimester; and so on. Travel days are printed in bold characters.

I. IV. VII. X. II. V. VIII. XI. III. VI. IX. XII.

A	1	8	*15*	22	29		6	13	20	27		4	*11*	18	25: Wed.
B	2	9	*16*	23	30		7	14	21	28		5	12	19	26: Thurs.
C	3	*10*	*17*	24		1	8	*15*	22	29		6	*13*	20	27: Fri.
D	4	11	18	25		2	9	16	23	30		7	14	21	28: *Sat.*
E	5	12	19	26		3	10	17	24		*1*	8	15	22	29: Sun.
F	6	*13*	20	27		4	11	18	25		2	9	*16*	23	30: Mon.
G	7	*14*	*21*	28		5	12	19	26		3	10	17	24	31: Tues.

The only day of the week on which no journey takes place is day D, the day on which also occurs the halt in the pursuit of Jacob by Laban. This is, consequently, the *sabbath*. Day A, which is the first day of each trimester and of the year falls on a *Wednesday*.[19]

A third approach could have been used by those authors who place the Feast of Weeks on a Sunday, if they had drawn up the above table. For if 15/III, thus day E, is a Sunday, day A still falls on a Wednesday.[20]

The table obtained in this way is most instructive and is fundamental to our present enquiry. In it may be ascertained immediately the *days of the liturgical festivals*:

Pasch	15/I	WEDNESDAY
Feast of Weeks (Pentecost)	15/III	SUNDAY
Day of Expiations	10/VII	FRIDAY
Feast of Tabernacles	15/VII	WEDNESDAY

Beginning (first day) of each month:

1/I	1/IV	1/VII	1/X	WEDNESDAY
1/II	1/V	1/VIII	1/XI	FRIDAY
1/III	1/VI	1/IX	1/XII	SUNDAY

We have deliberately avoided the term "new moon" for the first day of the month, since this designation can occasion confusion. In fact, it is only by way of exception that the beginning of the month in *Jubilees* can be a new moon. The Latin translation of *Jubilees* has always *primo (prima) die*.

A glance at the table shows that the days of the week brought into prominence by the liturgical calendar of *Jubilees* are Wednesday, Friday and Sunday, with special emphasis being laid on Wednesday. Wednesday is the day of the Pasch, of the Feast of Tabernacles and its octave (22/VII), of the four first days of the trimesters which are days of remembrance (Jub., 6,23-28). It is of decisive importance that the fragments of calendar 4Q give the dates of the liturgical festivals as days of the week. Furthermore, the days given correspond exactly to those of the above calendar table. The paschal sacrifice is assigned to a *Tuesday* because the Pasch is eaten in the evening of 14.[21]

A further glance at the list of journeys of the patriarchs will show that the dates explicitly mentioned by the author are in a direct relation with these "liturgical" days. The four first days of the trimesters are represented (Jub., 27,19; 31,3; 33,1; 45,1); and these fall on Wednesday. The intervention of Mastemah and the journey of Abraham are in direct relation to the Pasch. All the other dates fall on a Wednesday, a Friday, or a Sunday, with the exception of Jub., 29,5 (21/I, Tuesday) — but 21/I is the seventh day of the Pasch — and the further exception of Jub., 44,8 (16/III, Monday) — but the departure of Jacob takes place on the day after the Feast of Weeks. Even this account of the patriarchs' journeys, accordingly, is seen to be liturgical in character.

Let us now extend our enquiry to dates in the book other than those referring to the journeys of the patriarchs.[22]

Jubilees		Dates	
3,17	Temptation of Eve by the serpent	17/II	Sun.
3,32	Adam and Eve leave Paradise	1/IV	Wed.
7,2	Celebration of feast	1/I	Wed.
12,16	Abraham acknowledges the unique God	1/VII	Wed.
14,1	God speaks to Abraham	1/III	Sun.
15,1	Apparition to Abraham	15/III	Sun.
16,1	Apparition of angels	1/IV	Wed.
16,12	Conception of Isaac	15/VI	Sun.
16,13	Birth of Isaac	15/III	Sun.

We may break off here as the table is already sufficiently informative. The dates of the Flood have been deliberately omitted for the moment. First days of the trimesters still figure largely, the Feast of Weeks (15/III) holding the place of honor. Only Wednesday and Sunday occur in this partial list. If the sampling were carried further, a little more variety would be found in the dates: the mighty Abraham dies on the the day of the Feast of Weeks (Sunday) (Jub., 22,1); but Deborah, Rebecca's nurse, will have to be content with dying on a Thursday, 23/VII (Jub., 32,20), though it is true that it is the day following the octave of Tabernacles! The dates of birth of the patriarchs are distributed over several days of the week and it is not always easy to discover the purpose which has presided over the distribution; but it is certainly not by chance that Levi, whose role is a principal one in *Jubilees,* is born on 1/I, a Wednesday, as is Kaath in the *Testament of the XII Patriarchs.* Juda, like Isaac, is born on the Feast of Weeks, the festival of the Alliance (Sunday). For Joseph, whose figure assumes larger dimensions in the Jewish Haggada, is reserved the first day of month IV (Wednesday).[23]

These examples suffice to demonstrate that the principal events of the history of Israel are associated with the liturgy. In the mentality which presides over the drawing up of these accounts the history of the holy people is rendered sacred throughout. It is adapted to *the rhythm of a liturgical cycle.*

The question then arises: what is the origin of this sacred concept of history? What are the sources of such a calendar?

CHAPTER II

ORIGIN AND HISTORY OF
THIS ANCIENT CALENDAR

CERTAIN preliminary remarks must be made before we attempt to discover the origin of this calendar. First of all, there is the *internal evidence* of the texts. *Jubilees* and the documents of Qumran, as we have seen, lay down that, in order to return to the Law of Moses, in order to practice it in all its rigor, it is necessary to observe the festivals of the Alliance which were given by God to Moses and are written on the tables of the heavens. This is to say that, for the mentality of *Jubilees* and Qumran, this calendar had been imposed by Moses himself. It formed part of those venerable traditions which were held to go back to Henoch, which belonged to the sacred body of revelation handed down to Levi and his sons. However varied in character these affirmations may be, they all agree in stating that this calendar was a legacy from Israel's past.

Were it not for the great importance attached to problems of the calendar by the primitive mind, particularly in Judaism, and were it not for the polemical works given over entirely by this stern sect of pious Jews to the defense of this calendar[1]—works which were faithfully recopied—then it might be possible to question their good faith, or rather to suppose that the calendar was a work of artifice, the fruit of an unrealistic imagination. But the texts prove abundantly that this calendar was for them, at least throughout a whole period of their history, a matter of vital importance on which depended their faithfulness to the law of Moses. To abandon this calendar was to "walk in imitation of the Gentiles"; it was as bad as to "partake of the blood" (Jub., 6,38). This calendar must have possessed for them serious proofs of its authenticity.

One indication of ancient tradition is to be found in the date of the *Feast of Weeks,* assigned to a *Sunday,* the day after the sabbath. This is in fact the most natural interpretation of Lev., 23,6:

> "You shall count fifty days even unto the morrow after the seventh sabbath and so you shall offer a new sacrifice to the Lord."

On this point the tradition of *Jubilees,* in harmony here with that of the Samaritans, appears much more faithful than the Pharisee calendar.

It is to be noted finally that *Jubilee's* method of designating the months by *numerals* is characteristic of those biblical documents assigned by the critics to the priestly school. The texts, themselves, accordingly, lead us to examine in what measure these "sons of Levi, Sadoc and Aaron"[2] preserved a calendar proper to priestly documents.

The method to be followed is based on that suggested by the study of *Jubilees*. We shall translate into days of the week all the dates of the *Hexateuch* which are expressed by the *numerals of days and months*. We shall pass over the dates of festivals of the yearly liturgical cycle which have already been met with in *Jubilees* and which are exactly the same, thus giving the same results: *Wednesday, Friday, Sunday*.

Gen., 7,11	Beginning of the Flood	17/II	Sun.
Gen., 8,4	Ark comes to rest on Mt. Ararat	17/VII	Fri.
Gen., 8,5	Peaks of the mountains appear	1/X	Wed.
Gen., 8,13	The waters leave the earth to dry	1/I	Wed.
Gen., 8,14	The earth is dry	27/II	Wed.
Ex., 12,3	Choice of the paschal lamb	10/I	Fri.
Ex., 12,31-51	Departure from Egypt	15/I	Wed.
equals Num., 33,3			
Ex., 16,1	Arrival in desert of Sin	15/II	Fri.
Ex., 40,1-17	Building of tabernacle	1/I	Wed.
Num., 1,1	Numbering of children of Israel	1/II	Fri.
Num., 9,11	Pasch of second month (day after eating the lamb).	15/II	Fri.
Num., 10,11	Departure from Sinai	20/II	Wed.
Num., 33,38	Death of Aaron	1/V	Fri.

| Deut., 1,3 | Discourse of Moses | 1/XI | Fri. |
| Jos., 4,19 | Arrival in promised land | 10/I | Fri. |

It must be granted that it is difficult to attribute to chance results such as these which are so remarkably close to those of *Jubilees*.[3] The liturgical days are the same. There is the same preference for the first day of the month. There is the same respect for the sabbath rest; arrivals (including that of the ark on Mt. Ararat) take place on Friday, the vigil of the sabbath. There existed, then, in the priestly code, as in *Jubilees*, the law of abstention from travel on the sabbath day.

We may add a remark on the interpretation of Num., 10,33 which may be better explained by applying this calendar:

"They moved on from the mountain of the Lord, a three days' journey, and the Ark of the Covenant of the Lord which was to seek out their resting place went the three days' journey with them."

Whether or not one suppresses as a doublet the second mention of three days, the reference to 11 of the same chapter — even though the verses are separated by interjections — indicates that the three days are to be counted from the departure from Sinai on 20/III, a Wednesday. The three days of March are thus Wednesday, Thursday, Friday; the ark seeks a place of rest for Saturday, the sabbath day.

The much controverted question of the *chronology of the Flood* in document P may be interpreted, in light of this calendar, in the following fashion. The Flood begins on 17/II. The waters rise for 150 days (Gen., 7,24), and when, at the end of 150 days, they begin to subside, the ark comes to rest on Mt. Ararat on 17/VII (Gen., 8,4), thus *five months* after the beginning of the Flood. It follows that the total of the days of these five months must be *at least* equal to 150 days. Yet the sum of five lunar months would come to no more than a total of 147 or 148 days; consequently the hypothesis of lunar months must be eliminated. On the contrary, according to the calendar of *Jubilees,* between 17/II and 17/VII there occur three months of 30 days and two of 31 days; total: 152 days. The waters begin to subside at the end of 150 days — that is, on 15/VII, a *Wednesday* — and two days later, *Friday,* the vigil of the sabbath, the ark comes to rest on Mt. Ararat.[4]

The *Hexateuch,* in its priestly parts, provides a specially apt field for verifying our hypothesis, for in it ideal dates are projected onto the history of origins. But let us continue with the *Books of Paralipomenon* which, being of priestly origin, might be supposed to contain equally idealized history.

No date occurs in *Paralipomenon* which is contrary to the calendar of *Jubilees,* in the sense that no servile work and no journey is assigned to the sabbath day.[5] Only one date might weaken our hypothesis. In *II Par.,* 3,2, Solomon begins construction of the Temple on 2/II, which is a sabbath day. However, though the mention of month II is certain, the "second day" is missing in three Hebrew manuscripts, LXX, the Vulgate and the Syriac (cf. Begrich, Kittel ed.).

In *Esdras-Nehemias* we leave out of account dates expressed with the Babylonian names of the months. The list of the others runs:

Esd.,	7,9	Departure from Babylon	1/I	Wednesday
		Arrival at Jerusalem	1/V	Friday
Esd.,	8,31	Departure from the Ahava	12/I	Sunday
Esd.,	10,9	Gathering	20/IX	Friday
Esd.,	10,16	Beginning of session	1/X	Wednesday
Esd.,	10,17	End of session	1/I	Wednesday
Neh.,	8,2	Gathering	1/VII	Wednesday
Neh.,	9,1	Day of penance	24/VII	Friday

All the dates fall once more on *Wednesday* and *Friday*, with the exception of the departure from the Ahava which takes place on *Sunday*, the day after the sabbath. Arrival at Jerusalem is on Friday, the day before a sabbath. Once again, the first days of the "seasons" are given a place of honor.

The affinities between the *Book of Ezechiel* and the priestly code are well-known. In addition, the influence of Ezechiel on the sectaries of Qumran is beyond dispute. It is they who fulfill the word of the prophet, they, the sons of Sadoc, who have mounted guard over the santuary while the sons of Israel have gone astray, they who offer fat and blood (Ez., 44,15. CDC III 21-IV 2). Particularly close to Ezechiel is their vision of the restoration of the Temple.[6] Now, in the *Book of Ezechiel,* visions and prophecies, when they are dated, are done so in the fashion characteristic of the priestly code, always with the systems of numerals. The list of dates is as follows:

Ezechiel	*Oracles and visions*	*Dates*	
1,1	First vision	5/IV	Sunday
3,15-16	Seven days later	12/IV	Sunday

8,1	Vision		
	(T.M. 5/VI Thursday)		
	Cod. Petropol. (year 916)	1/VI	Sunday
	(LXX 5/V Tuesday)		
20,1	Oracle to ancients	10/V	Sunday
24,1	Against Jerusalem	10/X	Friday
	(cf. II Kings 25,1; Jer., 52,4)		
26,1	Against Tyre (1 of month)	1/?	W-F-S[7]
29,1	Against Egypt	12/X	Sunday
29,17	New oracle	1/I	Wednesday
30,20	Against Pharaoh	7/I	Tuesday
31,1	New oracle	1/III	Sunday
32,1	New oracle	1/XII	Sunday
32,17	New oracle	15/?	W-F-S
	(LXX 15/I Wednesday)		
33,21-23	Arrival of fugitive[8]	5/X	Sunday
	(LXX 5/XII Thursday)		
40,1	Vision of future Temple, 10th		
	day of *Rosh hashana*[9]	10/VII	Friday

Taking into account the difficulties of textual transmission, this table is not without a certain eloquence. Why is there this preference for Sunday? Are we here coming into contact with the roots of a symbolism of the first day of the week? In Ez., 8,1 we have opted for a date which in itself is uncertain. In Ez., 30,20, the only date which, being a Tuesday, "clashes" with the others, is 7/I; however, according to Ez., 45,20, this is a day of sacrifice. Is there trace here of a liturgical evolution?[10]

Apart from the dates assigned the visions and prophecies of Ezechiel, another argument—internal to the book itself

— supports our linking it with the calendar of *Jubilees*. The fourfold division of space, referred to in several passages of Ezechiel,[11] directs attention towards a division of time into four seasons; for the four parts of the sky traversed by the sun are precisely what define the four seasons of the year.[12] Perhaps it might be shown that the four living creatures of the vision of ch. 1, which indicate the four cardinal points, stand for four constellations separated from one another by an angle of 90°, as is admitted for the corresponding vision in the *Apocalypse*.[13]

In conclusion, after examination of the priestly texts, with which *Jubilees,* the *Writing of Damascus,* and the documents of Qumran present such remarkable affinities, the harmony as regards the calendar is too striking to permit rejection of the evidence supplied by the texts themselves that they preserve an ancient calendar of Israel. So many similarities cannot be due to mere chance. We are thus led to conclude that there exists a *continuity of calendar.* This does not mean that there could not have been a certain evolution or that additions or new interpretations could not have been introduced; in particular, the method of intercalating with the purpose of keeping in step with the solar year may have varied. It may also be assumed that various means were found to accomodate the calendar to the lunar system (Appendix III). But on one side and on the other is found the same distribution of days of the week with respect to days of the month; there is the same care to give special significance to certain liturgical days, in every case the same ones. The Jubilees-Qumran calendar is thus substantially the same as that of the priestly school.

Might it be possible to go back even further? What is

the reason for the importance — at first sight so surprising — of these liturgical days? For what reasons were they brought into prominence in this fashion? It is undoubtedly permissible to advance a *hypothesis of their origin*.

The importance attributed to these various days appears to be a direct consequence of the place that they occupy in the *sabbatical week*. Sunday, the first day of the week, the day after the sabbath, is the day of departure and of new undertakings.[14] Friday, the day before the sabbath, is the day of arrivals and of the assemblies which precede the sabbath.[15] Friday (the parasceve) would thus owe its importance to its place at the conclusion of the active days of the week and to the fact that it is the day of preparation for the sabbath. There remains the principal role assigned to Wednesday. Ought the importance granted the fourth day be attributed to the extremely ancient Oriental mystique of the number four? (Cf. the four parts of the world, the four winds, the four points of the compass, the four streams of paradise...).[16] What influence was the author of the first page of *Genesis* obeying when he placed the creation of the stars on the fourth day? If one remains on the level of the week, the importance of the fourth day appears to be due to the central position which it occupies in the week, equidistant from the two extremes.[17] It is quite possible that the various days presented a propitious or unpropitious character in the fashion of certain days of the month in the Babylonian calendar.[18] In any hypothesis, the manner in which the first, fourth and sixth days are presented appears to indicate that they are linked with the question of the sabbatical week and thus with the obscure origins of the sabbath.

Since it is certain that the week, as a unit of time, pre-

ceded the calendar of 364 days, it is entirely possible that
the privileged days of the week are likewise prior to it. The
research of Lewy has brought to light a calendar based on
a 50-day period, said to have existed in the East at a very
early epoch.[19] Although it is exceptionally difficult to recon-
struct a continuous calendar based on such a unit, it is certain at least that the period of fifty days existed as a unit of
time in the ancient East.[20] Now the basis of this 50-day
period — as the major unit — was the week — the minor unit.
The particularly stable character of the week as a fundamental unit of time, leads one to think that it persevered
through several quite distinct manners of reckoning, always
carrying with it its privileged days. It is in this fashion that
it would have entered as a basic unit into the priestly and
Jubilee reckoning: into the "quarter year" of 13 weeks and
into the year of 364 days which provided the best way of
combining a solar calendar with a pre-existing week. This
reckoning took as its point of departure the Wednesday, this
being certainly in conscious harmony with the priestly account of creation.

In any case, and whatever be the value of this reconstruc-
tion, it is certain that this *date of Wednesday*, which first
appeared as a distinctive characteristic of the Magarya, *is in
no sense an eccentric doctrine* in the Jewish tradition. Wednesday, the fourth day, was the day on which the stars were
created; it was logical to make it the point of departure for
their planetary revolutions. There exist witnesses to this tradition which, though late, belong to distinct areas of Judaism,
for they are found not only in the *Pirke Rabbi Eliezer*
(Palestinian tradition) but also in the Babylonian Talmud
and in Al-Biruni in a context wholly different from that of

the Magarya. These texts inform us of the existence in Judaism of a solar cycle which, every 28 years, started afresh at the spring equinox *at the beginning of the night between Tuesday and Wednesday* (see App. II). Even today, there is given in the Jewish ritual a blessing of the sun every 28 years on the first Wednesday of Nisan.[21] However obscure may be the origin of this cycle, we may retain the single element which interests us: the beginning on Wednesday.

The variety of witnesses to this manner of reckoning — at the same time as the distinctive character of this doctrine with respect to the rabbinical calendar where the year can never begin on a Wednesday — already leads one to conclude to an ancient origin. But comparison with the Jubilees-Magarya reckoning obliges us to push back this origin still further, for it is impossible to allow that a purely sectarian calendar could have given birth to talmudic traditions and perpetuated itself in a liturgy. It is, accordingly, necessary to ascend higher to a common doctrine, antecedent to the *Book of Jubilees,* and this is something which is perfectly in harmony with biblical origins. In this way, by another procedure, we find proof that a calendar, widely diffused in Judaism, began on a Wednesday at the spring equinox, at the very least before the middle of the second century.

This confirms the results which we have already obtained, but it does not yet prove that the rekoning was on an annual basis. For the commencement of each year on Wednesday, 1/I, presupposes a year of 364 days, exactly divisible by seven.

Evidence of a year of 364 days is already to be found in an important form of the *Slav Henoch.*[22] What is interesting about this reckoning is that it is not simply a borrowing from the Ethiopian Henoch, since it calculates differently the number of days in the months. It calculates them in two ways: according to the course of the sun, and according to that of the moon. The course of the sun results in a half-year composed of one month of 42 days and four of 35 days (total: 182 days). Thus here each month contains an exact number of weeks! Consequently, each month begins on the same day of the week — a curious advance on *Jubilees* and *I Henoch* which were content with a new beginning every three months, yet, at the same time, evidence of a like desire to give prominence to the same days of the week. As for reckoning based on the course of the moon, it is so eccentric that one might wonder whether a second solar reckoning were not being employed, for it too works out to 364 days.[23] The fantastic speculations of the Slav *Henoch* indicate that at the period, and in the climate of thought in which the book was composed, the priestly computation of the months had been abandoned, but that an attempt was being made to preserve the fixed postion in the year of the liturgical festivals. This point should be kept in mind.

Much useful documentation is to be found in the studies of Poznanski. He quotes the sectarian, Meswi al-Okhbari (second half of the ninth century) who affirmed that the Pasch must be held on a Thursday:

"so that the *Day of Expiations* may fall on a Saturday, and thus truly be a sabbath of sabbaths."

Now, this is possible only in a calendar of 364 days.[24] It is sufficient to postpone by one day the reckoning of *Jubilees* for the Feast of Kippur, which falls there on a Friday, to be transferred to the Saturday. This "rectification," if one may term it such, can be explained only in the perspective of our calendar and it appears to be a reaction against celebrating the Pasch on a Wednesday.

There is a further piece of evidence relative to *Wednesday* collected by Poznanski. According to Bar-Hebraeus, a certain Daniel, a disciple of the Karaite, Anan, had profaned the sabbath and made Wednesday the sacred day. Now, in a manuscript fragment published by Harkavy, a certain Al-Matari, who has been tentatively identified with the Daniel just mentioned, asserted that the festival of the seventh day ought to take place on Tuesday since, according to Gen., 1,14, the reckoning of days begins on a Wednesday.[25] This squares exactly with the reckoning of *Jubilees,* according to which the festival of the seventh day of the Pasch necessarily falls on a Tuesday.

Traces are thus found of the 364-day calendar both in the milieu of the Slav *Henoch* and among the Karaites.[26] Clearly, they are no more than traces, yet it is not without significance when they are to be discovered in such widely differing ambients. They provide evidence suggesting a fairly widespread base at the origin of the tradition.

An attempt must now be made to marshal the data available for sketching out a *history of the ancient priestly calendar,* beginning with the biblical documents up to the moment of its disintegration. There is no question of presenting here a finished account of the Israelite calendar, a task which the scarcity of information would render difficult in the extreme. Areas of agreement are rare in this subject: the material is so uncertain and the data so tenuous that we are left in a state of perplexity when it comes to interpretation of texts and to the overlapping of the solar and the lunar calendars.[27] Our aim is more modest. We shall restrict ourselves to the post-Exilic period, developing elsewhere the special problems of the lunar question (Appendix III), and seeking here to assemble information rather than construct a systematic exposition.

Firstly, there is the *internal* approach to the problem. This consists in applying to the other books of the Bible the table of conversion into days of the week which has already been used for the priestly documents and for Ezechiel.

The *Books of Kings* employ very ancient names of the month used in Israel (Bul, Ziv, Ethanim). A few dates, however, are given with the numerals of the days and months. In *I Kings*, 12,32-22, Jeroboam establishes in the Kingdom of Israel a festival on 15/VII, in competition with Juda's festival. This feast falls on a Friday. Two other important dates are noted for Friday: the siege of Jerusalem, 10/X (*II Kings*, 25,1; Jer., 52,4; Ez., 24,1) and the release of Joachim, 27/XII (*II Kings*, 25,27; Jer., 52,31). The manuscript tradition is hesitant on the dates of the capture and the burning of Jerusalem.[28]

Few dates expressed in numerals are to be found in the prophets. The dates of *Aggeus* are not opposed to the priestly calendar.[29] The only two dates of *Zachary* are fully in harmony, for they are a Sunday and a Wednesday: 24/XI — which is the month of Shebat (Zach., 1,7); and 4/IX — in Kislev (Zach., 7,1). The dates are particularly interesting by reason of Zachary's priestly associations and because the months are expressed according to the Babylonian system.[30]

Coming to a later period, we find a single date in *Daniel*:

24/I, Friday (Dan., 10,4); in *Judith* only one: 22/I, Wednesday (Jud., 2,1).[31]

Apart from the special case of Aggeus and a few doubtful dates in the *Books of Kings,* it is certain that all the "numerical" dates fall on *one of three liturgical days.* There is little doubt that this is not a matter of chance; nevertheless, prudence is indicated in the interpretation of such meager evidence.

The case of *I Machabees* is far from simple. While the text on the entry of Simon into the castle of Jerusalem (13,51) on 23/II, a sabbath, raises a certain difficulty,[32] the festival of the restoration of the Temple, mentioned in 4,52, begins on 25/IX (Wednesday and ends eight days later, thus also on a Wednesday. When 18 Elul, the date of the great declaration graven on table of brass, is converted into 18/VI, it may be seen that it falls on a Wednesday (I Mac., 14,27). In 7,4 the Jews' pursuit of the enemy lasts one day; the date was 13 Adar or 13/XII (Friday). Does not this suggest that a halt was called when the sabbath began? It is not impossible, accordingly, that one of the principal sources utilized by the editor of *I Machabees* still bore evidence of employment of our calendar.[33]

The texts just considered, belonging as they do to a later period, authorize speculations rather than firm conclusions. They suggest that certain religious groups had remained attached to the ancient priestly calendar in the first half of the second century. Moreover, given the number of dates expressed in the Babylonian style, and given the testimony of Sirach (see App. III), it is probable that a gradual modification of the ancient priestly system was introduced, at first under Babylonian influence, then, during the course of the

45

third century, under the growing influence of Hellenism. At the same time, this intermediary calendar could well have remained to a considerable degree dependent on the ancient system, maintaining the feasts on the day of the week traditionally assigned to them (see Appendix III). Too abrupt a scheme of Hellenization at the time of Antiochus Epiphanes, who wished to:

"change the *times* and the law" (Dan., 7,25)

would appear to have precipitated a crisis which doubtless remained beneath the surface. The Assideo-Machibean uprising could have been due in part to a dispute over the calendar. The "conservatives"— whose views are voiced in the *Book of Jubilees* — would then have returned to the integral calendar which God had revealed and which "the whole of Israel" had abandoned. The expressions appearing in *Jubilees* and in the *Writing of Damascus* do, in fact, appear to indicate that a certain dissatisfaction with this calendar had shown itself. Nevertheless, the descendants of the Asmoneans would have permitted a process of evolution which terminated in the system with which we are familiar.

Turning our attention to *external* evidence, we come once again to Al-Biruni.

The following curious passage occurs in a chapter in which the author discusses intercalations and the method for determining the new moon:

"Prior to that time (200 years after Alexander), they (the Jews) were accustomed to observe the *tequfoth*, that is, the quarter-years (solstices or equinoxes)...and to compare them with the conjunction of the month to which a particular *tequfah* ought to have corresponded. If they found that the conjunction preceded the *tequfah* by about thirty days, they intercalated a month that year. For example, if they found that the conjunction of Tammuz preceded the *tequfah* of Tammuz, that is, the summer solstice, by about thirty days, they intercalated that year another month of Tammuz, with the result that there was a First Tammuz and a Second Tammuz. They dealt in like manner with the other *tequfoth*."[34]

Two hundred years after Alexander brings us towards 150-125 B.C. — that is, if the figure is correct! In any case, the statement is extremely important in the light of what we know of the four seasons of the ancient calendar. It confirms that, up to nearly the middle of the second century B.C., the greater part of Judaism took account of observation of the solstices and equinoxes. This leads us to suppose that, in the 364-day calendar, intercalations were inserted between the different quarter-years — hence the signficance of the first days of each season. Since, however, the addition of thirty intercalary days was not admissible under our calendar, it is likely that Al-Biruni is referring to a lunar calendar (notice the Babylonian name: Tammuz) which still remains close to the ancient system and in which special significance is attributed to the four *seasons*. This supposition provides the best explanation for the complaint of *Jubilees* against the moon which "upsets the season."[35] Such dates as are supplied by Al-Biruni are fully in harmony with our evolutionary hypothesis as a whole.

In another place Al-Biruni draws up a list of days on which, according to the Jewish calendar, certain annual festivals cannot fall. He notes that Tishri 1 cannot fall on the first, fourth or sixth day of the week. Kippur is excluded from the first, third and sixth days and the Pasch from the second, fourth and sixth days. The reason for this, he goes on, is that it is necessary to avoid two consecutive days of rest or a sabbath coinciding with the vigil of a festival which requires preparation.

"This is why an attempt has been made to construct a calendar in which one day of rest does not follow immediately on another."[36]

Now, under the ancient system, 1/VII always falls on the fourth day, the Pasch on the fourth day, and Kippur on the sixth day, all of these, days *prohibited* by the common Jewish calendar to which Al-Biruni refers. It is precisely in this context that the famous remark about the Magarya finds its place. This group is singled out for explicit mention because it ignored the law by celebrating the Pasch on a Wednesday. It seems that we are encountering here an important point of friction between the calendar of *Jubilees* and the official calendar. At the same time we are presented with one of the reasons for the opposition set up to the ancient priestly calendar. When it is remembered that according to the reckoning of the priestly calendar, the liturgical festivals fell on the first, fourth and sixth days, it will be easy to understand how great a revolution was involved in the introduction of the law concerning two successive days of rest. The sole motive that could be invoked was a sacred one: the protection of the sabbath. Those who supported the "legal" calendar wished only to avoid profanation of the holy day.

48

The Ancient Jewish Calendar

The contrast of opinion was never more clearly formulated, the clash never more bitter, than when the partisans of the calendar based on the lunar month, not content with giving the day of the month priority over the day of the week, went so far as to outlaw the days hallowed by tradition. They claimed that they were acting in defense of the sabbath and preserving the traditional system of dates which they were simply adapting to the lunar month. There were several excellent reasons in their favor; nevertheless, the traditional system, based on the week, was to be perpetuated in circles which were attached to ancient traditions, though not sharing the extreme conservatism of *Jubilees*. It is easy to understand why this book anathematized those who had substituted the impure day for the pure day, the profane day for the sacred day. If this is, in fact, the explanation of the outraged protests voiced by *Jubilees*, then this highly significant cleavage of opinion would have to be placed before 125 at the latest.

Finally, the clearest contrast between the official and the "unofficial" calendars is that between *movable* and *fixed feast-days*. Yet, in addition to this, there appears to have been introduced at a very early date a *differentiation* as regards the days of the week. This is of special interest for our attempt to determine the date of the *Pasch*. Certain sectors, however, were affected only at a later period. *Pentecost* was for long to remain fixed on Sunday, as is proved by the claims which are preserved in the Mishna and the Talmud (see p. 23 above). It is difficult to determine precisely the period. Under John Hyrkan, Pentecost was celebrated at least once on a Sunday (*A.J.* XIII 8,4); but this could be simply coincidence. According to Derenbourg, the "re-establishment" of the Feast of Weeks, together with the forbidding of mourning on Megil-

49

lath Taanith, represented a victory of the Pharisees over the Sadducees and their manner of celebrating the feast.[37] But the law excluding two consecutive days of rest was never applied to Pentecost. This indicates that Sunday, assigned since earliest times to the Feast of Weeks, put up solid resistance to any change. This was no doubt due to its occurring on the fiftieth day, the day after seven sabbaths. This gave it a stability which permitted it to maintain its existence even in methods of calculation which had abandoned the priestly system of reckoning and had adopted the lunar months. There is little doubt that Pentecost was linked by its origins more to the period of fifty days than to the 364-day calendar.[38] It offers a typical example of the way in which the liturgical days of the week could enjoy in Judaism a greater stability than the 364-day calendar.

Towards the beginning of the Christian era very clear and trustworthy evidence of the observance of the days of the week is to be found in the circles of Qumran and related writings. According to information which Mr. Milik was kind enough to give me orally, the manuscripts of the liturgical calendar of 4Q generally show a hand of "Herodian" type (end of the first century, B.C. and beginning of the first century, A.D.). Even if we are dealing here with a copy, it proves that interest in assigning festivals to fixed days of the week had not diminished.[39] According to a source utilized by the *Testaments of the XII Patriarchs,* Kaath was born on 1/I (Wednesday) at sun-rise.[40] In the *Greek Testaments* Nephtal assembled his children on 1/VII (Wednesday).[41] These are the clearest cases. In other works, in which literary affinities are discernible, there remain nothing more than vestiges.[42]

It is quite reasonable to suppose that, in later Judaism, the priestly reckoning was no longer in current usage (if, indeed, it ever had been). It survived only in the liturgical usage of certain circles and as an archaism. Hence the importance of the chance discovery of a ritual, or rather of narrative texts, which indirectly betray, through the projection of holy days onto their account of the sacred history of the past, the liturgical customs of these circles. The various official calendars could only show the commonly used dates. Such is the case with the *Machabees* and later with Josephus. At Qumran itself, certain historical events, commemorated in the customary calendar of the sect, are dated in the way of the current calendar according to the Babylonian system.[43]

It will, accordingly, be seen how difficult it is to establish for the Judaism of the time of Christ a "map" of the calendar which would indicate the extent of use of the ancient priestly calendar. To complicate the matter further, there are several good reasons for thinking that there existed a *modified calendar* which had been adapted to the phases of the moon, yet still preserved the same days of the week for liturgical feasts (Appendix III). A calendar of this kind may have been in existence at the period of Sirach. The hesitancy in locating the Sunday of Pentecost, the abandonment of the numeral system in the Slav *Henoch*, the "lunar" preoccupations of *I Henoch* and certain texts which give evidence of a solar cycle beginning on a Wednesday, all point in the same direction. Further, it is not beyond the bounds of historical likelihood that centers following their usage had jealously preserved the venerable traditions placing liturgical celebrations on fixed days of the week, and yet, at the same time, for the sake of not separating themselves too far from the liturgy of the

Temple, had attempted a compromise, celebrating their own feasts on a fixed day close to the date of the official feast. In this fashion, the feasts would coincide at least during the octave.

In conclusion: it is certain that, at the beginning of the first century, A.D., there existed *two liturgical calendars*. In one of these the feasts were assigned to days of the lunar month; this was the official calendar, about which we can find information in later rabbinical Judaism. In the second, the feasts always fell on fixed days of the week. The character of this calendar may now be discovered in contemporary Jewish sources. It is witnessed only in its Jubilees-Qumran type; but it is probable that it also existed in modified forms which could have either preserved an intermediary stage of the calendar's development or attempted a certain compromise with the official reckoning.

At the period in which we are interested, the second calendar is purely a liturgical one and is an archaic usage. It is to be found only in isolated circles; and it seems to be on the point of disappearing. Yet, and this is the important point, it is destined to survive itself within the vast movement of early Christianity. The true success of this calendar is the Christian liturgy.

CHAPTER III

AT THE SOURCES OF THE CHRISTIAN LITURGY

T HE first indications of liturgical dates appear in the
Didache:

"Your fasts must not take place at the same time as those
of the hypocrites. They fast on Monday and Thursday;
you are to fast on Wednesday and Friday" (Did., 8,1).

The earliest Christian "calendar," accordingly, is characterized
by its *opposition to the days of the week* observed by the
"hypocrites," that is, the Pharisees. The Christian days are
Wednesday and *Friday*. To these must be added *Sunday*,

spoken of in the New Testament itself as the Lord's Day (Apoc., 1,10), and the day of the Eucharistic assembly (Acts 20,7).[1] Wednesday, Friday, Sunday, these are the liturgical days of the primitive Christian community. These, too, were those of the ancient priestly calendar, in contrast to the official calendar. It is difficult not to see in this a liturgical form of continuity.

Wednesday and Friday are days of fasting.[2] They are the days of the *statio,* a term whose meaning is certainly borrowed from Judaism and which translates the Hebrew, *ma'amad.* In the Talmud and the Mishna, this word signifies the liturgical services maintained in rote by the Temple guard.[3] They are likewise the days of the Eucharistic assembly, having their origin with the Apostles themselves.[4] At a very early age the fasts of Wednesday and Friday were connected with the passion of Jesus.[5] For the moment it is sufficient to notice this fact without seeking to explain the significance of Wednesday. As for the Sunday, it was observed at an early date in memory of the resurrection.

These three liturgical days, consequently, are found to have the character of memorial days in the early Church. There seems little doubt that they already possessed some particular aptitude for their new functions. It is probable, on the other hand, that the new significance assigned to them contributed to their being retained in the Christian liturgy. Now, this idea of commemoration was quite in harmony with the priestly documents and with the *Book of Jubilees.* It is interesting to find that it reappears in Christianity, because this indicates not only continuity of liturgical practice, but also continuity of that mentality for which the whole of sacred history unfolds according to a sacred rhythm.

We ask for indulgence if we consider first of all a Christian apocryphal work of Jewish origin which, though of rather childish character, supplies a straightforward application of the method of *Jubilees*. This work is entitled the *Book of Adam and Eve,* also known as *the Combat of Adam and Eve.*[6]

This apocryphal work, no longer existing except in its Ethiopian and Arabic translations, appears to date, in its present form, from the fifth or sixth century, A.D.; but it is obvious that the editor has made use of a broad fund of Jewish traditions which he collects, in his work. The first and longest part, which is the most relevant to our subject, relates the history of origins up to Abraham, insisting on the combats of Adam and Eve with the serpent and then on the legend of Melchisedech. The author notes the dates of several outstanding events, and fortunately he often does so in full, adding the day of the week. There follows a complete list of these dates; the page-numbers refer to the Malan edition:

A. — Adam was brought into paradise on a *Friday,* transgressed the commandment at the sixth hour and left at the ninth hour (pp. 37-41 and p. 116).

B. — "Adam died on 15 of the month Bermudah (after the calculation of the epact of the sun), at the ninth hour. It was a *Friday* when he died, the same day as that on which he was created. And the hour of his death was the same as that of his expulsion from the garden" (p. 116).

C. — Jared died on 12 of Takhsas, a *Friday* (p. 140).

D. — "The death of Methuselah took place on 12 of Magabit, a *Sunday*" (p. 150).

E. — Noah brought the body of Adam into the ark "on

a *Friday,* at the second hour of the day, 27 of the month Gembot" (p. 153).

On the same Friday took place the general boarding of the ark, at the third, sixth and ninth hours successively (p. 154).

F. — Noah left the ark "on the 27 of the month Gembot, a *Sunday"* (p. 158).

G. — "Noah died on a *Wednesday,* 2 of the month Gembot, on the mountain on which the ark rested" (p. 163).

To these may be added the sole date which is given in the numerals of day and month. "On the first day of month XI were seen the peaks of the mountains" (p. 157); 1/XI is a Friday. This is the text of LXX in Gen., 8,5. T.M. and *Jubilees* have 1/X, a Wednesday.

In these texts it is the turn of Friday to hold the principal position (A B C E), and stress is laid on the division of the day into liturgical hours, evidently with reference to the passion. Adam dies on Friday at the ninth hour (B) because of his typological function; throughout the book, Adam foreshadows Christ. The reference to the epact — that is, the intercalation which brings the calendar into harmony with the solar cycle — should be noticed. The belief that Adam left paradise on the same day that he entered is also found elsewhere (cf. Malan, p. 211) but is not in accord with the tradition of *Jubilees* which has Adam leaving paradise on a Wednesday, several years after he had entered it (Jub., 3,32).

In E, everyone entered the ark on the eve of the sabbath; it is probable that this was already the interpretation of *Jubilees.*[7]

56

Text F: in *Jubilees,* Noah left the ark on 1/III, likewise a Sunday, the beginning of the week (Jub., 6,1). In our text it is the 27th day of the month Gembot, which accords with G (Wednesday, 2), but not with E, where the same date falls on a Friday. In the system followed by the author, consequently, the same date of the month does not correspond to the same day of the week.[8]

This apocryphal work employs a curious enumeration of the days, which begins with the *Friday* when Adam and Eve went out of the garden. The bringing into relief of certain days may be accounted for on Christian grounds; nevertheless, the impression one receives is that the Christian interpretation was superimposed on an existing base of Jewish origin. The figures are sometimes contradictory and the numbering is not altogether free from confusion. The following are the most striking examples; we shall translate the numerals into days.

On the 3rd day after the expulsion from the garden — hence on a *Sunday* — God gives Adam a sign, by reason of the three days that Christ would remain in the womb of the earth (p. 33). On the 43rd day — thus a *Friday* — Adam begs God to forgive him, but these 43 days cannot redeem the hour in which he sinned (pp. 36-42). *Fifty* days pass since the expulsion from the garden — bringing us up to the *Friday,* inclusive — and then Adam and Eve must spend three days and nights under a rock in symbol of Christ's sojourn in the tomb (pp. 55-57). On the 92nd day — thus a *Friday* — towards the end of the day, Adam offers a great sacrifice upon which the Holy Spirit descends (p. 82). There follows a further period of 50 days — divided by the sacrifices of *Wednesday, Friday* and *Sunday* — which is completed with the offering of the first day (*Sunday*) which is also the 50th (p. 83), and "on this first day which is the term of 7 weeks and which is the 50th day" God heals Adam of the wounds inflicted by Satan (p. 84).

Attention must be drawn to the *two periods of 50 days* and particularly to the importance of the *92nd day* which, in *Jubilees*, is the day which begins a new quarter (the first day of a trimester). But in this Christian adaptation, the 92nd day — the original significance of which has been lost — is no longer a Wednesday, but a Friday. The sacrifice offered by Adam towards the end of this day evidently prefigures that of Calvary. Occasion will be found later to return to this text. For the moment, it is sufficient to notice the importance given throughout the period of fifty days to the three days of the Eucharistic assemblies: Wednesday, Friday and Sunday.

These very striking similarities with the *Book of Jubilees* are all the more interesting since they betray no direct literary influence;[9] yet the climate of thought is the same: *history is liturgy.* And this liturgy is none other than that of the old priestly calendar, with attention not turned from Wednesday to Friday because its center has become Christ, the one proclaimed by the whole of sacred history. Thus we have to do with a continuity and, at the same time, a transposition. Other texts will confirm this situation in early Christianity. In these, the liturgical days are projected onto the life of Christ.

The Armenian *Synaxary of Ter Israel* presents the following tradition for the date of 6 January:

"Thirty years later, on the same day, 6 January, a Sunday, Jesus came to the Jordan to be baptized by John. For he was *born* on a Thursday evening, just as *Friday*, the day of Adam's creation, was beginning. He was *announced* on a *Wednesday* and *baptized* on a *Sunday,* the day of creation and of his resurrection."[10]

The reason for placing Christ's birth on a Friday is clearly indicated. The new Adam was born on the same day that the first man was created. The *Book of Adam and Eve* has prepared us for this kind of symbolism.

The *Armenian Book of the Childhood* places the Annunciation on a Wednesday. But it is noticeable that this Wednesday is 15 Nisan.[11] This, evidently, is the day of the Pasch. When it is remembered that, in the official calendar, the Pasch could never fall on a Wednesday, it is difficult not to see here an echo of the old priestly calendar.

Another very early tradition places the *birth of Christ* on a *Wednesday.* This is found in the *Commentary on Daniel* of Hippolytus. This text has been the subject of considerable discussion, not as regards the day of the week, but as regards the date of 25 December, which appears to be an adjustment made by a later hand. The original date would seem to be a Wednesday at the beginning of April.[12] This latter date, placing Christ's birth in the springtime, is all the more likely since Hippolytus was familiar with a priestly tradition on Christ's birth.[13] Now, in *Jubilees,* Levi himself, and in the *Testaments,* his son Kaath, were born on 1/I, thus on Wednesday. This 1/I would appear to represent the ideal date of the creation of the sun at the beginning of spring, in harmony with the solar symbolism applied to the priestly Messiah.[14]

The Christian liturgy, which finally placed the Annunciation at the spring equinox (25 March), thus reserved for the birth of Christ a further solar symbolism, that is of the winter solstice (25 December). But the analogy of an explicit text of *De pascha computus* on the date of the Nativity leads one to think that the spring date represents a very early tradition. It will be recalled that, for the *De pascha computus,* the moon and the sun were created on Wednesday, five days before the kalends of April (28 March) (see Appendix III):

> "How wonderful and divine is the providence of the Lord: Christ was born on the day of the creation of the sun, Wednesday, 5 days before the kalends of April. Rightly did the prophet Malachy say to the people: The sun of justice shall rise for you."[15]

The writer's enthusiasm is only to be explained by an earlier tradition. And this tradition seems to flow directly from the date of birth of the Messiah, son of Levi, given in the *Testaments of the XII Patriarchs* and in *Jubilees*. It is explained by the importance given to Wednesday, 1/I, at the beginning of spring, in the priestly calendar. It will not be forgotten that in this calendar, 1/I is the date of the raising of the tabernacle, the day when Aaron and his sons were anointed, consecrated and clothed with the priestly power (Ex., 40,1-17). In the Syrian version of Num., 33, 38, the same date is assigned to the death of Aaron. This was a most holy date, beginning the year and freely chosen by the priest Esdras and his company for going up to Babylon (Esd., 7,9).[16] It was, accordingly, entirely suitable for being linked with the priestly power. Here we encounter a direct line leading from the priestly code to a Christological symbolism.

The affinities just described are not meant to be exhaustive.[17] But the examples cited suffice to prove an *undoubted continuity* between early Christianity and the Jewish circles who followed the old priestly calendar.

Yet this continuity of liturgical days is not the only indication of a transition from the former priestly ritual to the Christian ritual. The practice of *Quarter Tense,* the origins of which are so obscure, may be explained by the division of the old calendar into four seasons.

In the Christian, as in the old, calendar, Pentecost is fixed on a Sunday. Without any doubt it may be stated that, in the year when Christ died, the official Pentecost also fell on a Sunday, since the official Pasch took place on a Saturday. But what is striking in the Christian liturgy is precisely its preference of the day of the week to the day of the lunar month. Moreover, the calculation of the feast of Pentecost in the Church raises a new problem. For the Christian Pentecost is calculated from Easter Sunday, that is to say — in terms of the Jewish calendar — from the sabbath within the octave of the Pasch. According to the reckoning of *Jubilees,* on the contrary, it would be celebrated eight days later. This seems to be due to the influence of the official calendar.

The feast of *Easter* poses a similar problem. The Christian Easter is fixed on a Sunday — an example of preference for a day of the week rather than a date in the month; but this Sunday depends on the Easter moon, a method of reckoning which found no place in the old calendar, at least in the form in which we know this calendar (see Appendix III). In this case also the Christian calendar may have been the descendant of a modified form of the old calendar.

Also to be noted is the particular concern of Christian writers to stress the fact that the feast of Easter always falls after the spring equinox. They recall that such was the practice of the Jews who followed "a divine ordinance" when they sacrificed the Pasch after the equinox.[18] Condemnations of the most forceful kind are uttered against those who would celebrate Easter before the equinox, "as is the custom of the Jews"—evidently, contemporary Jews.[19] Such polemical remarks as these can only be explained by the Jewish reckoning of twelve lunar months with a supplementary month intercalated. Whenever the thirteenth month was not inserted early enough, it was possible that the 15 Nisan might fall before the spring equinox. In this matter, accordingly, Christians were conscious of having preserved the ancient custom based on observation of the spring equinox.

Finally, knowledge of the fixed-day calendar throws new light on the *Easter dispute* at the end of the second century. For the inhabitants of Asia Minor, Easter was determined by the date of the month, on whatever day of the week it might fall. In Rome and the other churches the traditional date was a Sunday. *The day of the week against the day of the lunar month*: this was the conflict already to be found in Judaism between the two calendars.

The bishops of Asia Minor pointed with emotion to the authorities guaranteeing the venerable and ancient character of their tradition; among these authorities were Polycarp and John.[20] They depended, consequently, upon the Johannine tradition which refers only to the official Pasch (we shall have occasion to explain this apparent anomaly). The other churches, on the contrary, followed the Sunday usage, in virtue, so Eusebius claims, of an apostolic tradition.[21] It is, in fact, sufficient to read the episcopal letters quoted by Eusebius in order to be convinced of the antiquity of the tradition of celebrating Easter on Sunday. The bishops of Palestine bear witness:

"to a tradition concerning Easter, handed down to them through the apostolic succession"

and they state that "those of Alexandria celebrate Easter on the same day."[22]

This agreement among the three churches of Palestine, Alexandria and Rome — to which, according to Eusebius, we should add Pontus and Osroene[23] — cannot fail to impress. What other reason may be assigned such agreement if not that Easter was originally celebrated on a fixed day, Sunday?

This dispute throws considerable light on the nature of the basic plan of the early Christian liturgy. Characteristic was the adoption of the practice of placing feasts on fixed days of the week, rather than on movable days, as was normal for the official calendar. In addition, by preserving the three basic days of the old calendar, the Christian liturgy was explicitly opposed to the official calendar. To account for this we must conclude that in the Jewish circles where early Christianity took shape, it was the old calendar which was principally followed.

This brings us to the question which is of primary interest for Christian origins: in what Jewish environment does early Christianity have its roots? The calendar conflict with the Jewish authorities of the nation can only lend confirmation to the conflict appearing on every page of the Gospel. As well, the old priestly calendar was observed at Qumran. Consequently, there were undoubted affinities, at least as to origin, between the disciples' community and the circles of Qumran

and of the Essenes. This is in harmony with the many similarities already established by qualified specialists between early
Christianity and the Qumran circle.

On this point, however, the calendar does not, at the
moment, shed as much light as one might have hoped. The
contrast between the fixed-day and the movable-day calendars must, indeed, have placed a deep gulf between official
circles and — the others. But, as far as the latter are concerned,
we do not know to what extent there existed modified forms
of which the tendency was to move closer to the lunar phases
and the official calendar. Up to the present the documents
preserved at Qumran and the analogy of *Jubilees* reveal only
a calendar which is integrally "orthodox," not to say integral-
ist. A text of Epiphanius, containing reference to the calendar
disputes among the Jewish sects, states that:

> "the Essenes had maintained the original usage, without
> any additions."[24]

Nevertheless, taking into account the entire Essenian movement, which must have been extremely complex, it is far
from impossible that certain adapted forms are yet to be discovered (Cf. App. III).

As regards early Christianity, and leaving aside the special
characteristics of the apostolic group and their relations with
the Temple, there is the absence of allusion in Christian
writers to the 364-day calendar; there is the calculation of
Pentecost from the sabbath within the octave, and the connection, to all appearances dating from the earliest period,
between Easter and the phases of the moon. All of this leads
one to think that Christianity had inherited a *modified form*

64

of calendar, a form which may well have gone back to the distant past as far as the intermediary types preceding the break with the circle of *Jubilees.* Here the problem becomes extremely complex, for, although many of the writings of Qumran found no acceptance in Christianity, it is certain that it is through Christian hands that the *Book of Jubilees* has been handed down to us. Certain supporters of this book, consequently, became Christians. If one thinks, moreover, of the very large number of Jewish apocrypha preserved in Christianity, one realizes the variety and the importance of the Jewish influences which won acceptance in the Christian movement. Thus in this matter of comparison, unless fresh discoveries are made, the principal method remains that of noting literary similarities in the various texts.

For our purpose, however, the essential point has been established. There exists *a fundamental continuity between the Jewish fixed-day calendar and the Christian calendar,* whatever lunar modifications may have been made. The stability of liturgical forms is well known. The apostolic group preserved the venerated days handed down to them by the old priestly calendar, merely giving them a new significance. And this being so, one consequence follows immediately: if the Jewish circles which gave birth to Christianity celebrated the festivals on fixed days, it must have celebrated the Pasch on Wednesday and the paschal meal on Tuesday evening.

It must be agreed that it would be singularly unusual if the Last Supper of Jesus, the meal around which the whole Christian liturgy revolves, had been celebrated in a manner opposed to the basic principles of that liturgy and outside the main-stream of that continuous development which led from one liturgy to the other. For the primitive community this

65

meal was central and normative. If the circle to which the disciples belonged used the fixed-day calendar, how could Jesus himself have celebrated the Pasch on any other day than Tuesday evening? Such is the conclusion which emerges of itself from the fact of continuity in the calendars.

Second Part

A Patristic Tradition

CHAPTER ONE

THE EVIDENCE

THE principal texts which bear witness to a tradition that the Supper was celebrated on Tuesday evening are to be found in the *Didascalia*.[1] Since its discovery, this work has been considered by the critics as a document of foremost value for knowledge of the ancient church. The *Didascalia* has been preserved in Syriac. The fidelity of this version may fortunately be verified by comparison with a fragment of a Latin translation. The composition of the *Didascalia* has been set in the third century; more precisely, if certain interpolations are admitted, at the beginning of this century.[2] Galtier is even inclined to move the date back to the second century; so too is Charles.[3]

The *Didascalia* belongs to that group of early writings, containing moral exhortation and Church legislation, which are attributed to the twelve Apostles: the *Didache*, the *Octateuch of Clement*, the *Canons of Hippolytus* .... The *Didascalia* was used, in its Greek form, by the *Apostolic Constitutions*. Like such related works, the *Didascalia* consists in a compilation which includes earlier documents, such as the *Prayer of Manassah*, Jewish in origin, of which the *Didascalia* is the first witness. Certain semitisms are to be found in the *Didascalia*.[4] Several critics have already been struck by the Judaeo-Christian ties of this work which specifically combats judaising tendencies.[5] It will certainly be necessary to reopen the study of this composition in the light of recent discoveries. Almost everywhere in it there appear literary affinities with Jewish circles of priestly outlook.[6]

Chapter 21, which is of special interest to us, is unusual. It begins, in harmony with the general tone of the work, with moral exhortations; but, then, in relation to the law of fasting, it reproduces narrative texts on the passion, containing a chronology of the week of the passion. Here the Supper is placed on Tuesday evening, the arrest takes place during the night between Tuesday and Wednesday, while the crucifixion is still fixed on the Friday.

It is necessary to reproduce large extracts from this chapter. The Apostles are represented as speaking.[7]

Didascalia, chapter 21.
X-XII,5. — [It is not licit for a Christian to swear or to utter vain or impure words; nothing should be spoken by

his lips but blessings] "especially during the days of the Pasch when all the faithful throughout the world fast"...

XIII. — "Further, when you fast, pray and intercede for those who have perished, just as we did when our Savior suffered."

XIV. — 1. "While he was still with us before his passion, when we were eating the Pasch with him, he said to us: Today, on this very night, one of you will betray me. And each one of us said to him: Will it be I, Lord? He answered and said to us: It is he who dips his hand in the plate with me. 2. And Judas Iscariot, who was one of us, rose up to betray him. 3. Then our Lord said to us: Truly I say to you: a little while and you shall abandon me, for it is written: I shall strike the shepherd and the lambs of his flock shall be scattered. 4. Judas came with the scribes and with the priests of the people and he delivered up our Lord Jesus. This took place on *Wednesday*. 5. After eating the Pasch, on *Tuesday* evening, we went to the Mt. of Olives and, in the night, they took our Lord Jesus. 6. The following day, which is *Wednesday*, he was kept in the house of the high priest, Caiphas; the same day the leaders of the people met and discussed his case. 7. The following day, Thursday, they brought him to the governor, Pilate, and he was kept with Pilate through the night following Thursday. 8. On the morning of the Friday they made many accusations concerning him before Pilate, but they could prove nothing against him, and they brought false witnesses against him, and they called upon Pilate to put him to death. 9. They crucified him that same Friday, and he suffered on Friday for six hours. These hours of our Lord's crucifixion are counted as one day. 10. There followed three hours of darkness; these (hours) are counted as one night. Then, from the ninth hour to evening, there were three hours of day; there followed the night of Saturday of the passion .... 12. There came the day of Saturday, and then three hours of the night after Saturday, during which Jesus slept (and rose). 13. Thus was fulfilled the word: The son of man must pass three days and three nights in the womb of the earth, as it is written in the Gospel. It is also written in David: Behold, thou hast disposed the days with measure. It is so written because these days and nights were shortened."

XIV,14-17. — [In an apparition to his disciples, Jesus asked them to fast on Wednesday and Friday, but they are not to fast on Sunday which will not be counted among the days of fast of the passion; during the time of his passion, they are to fast from Monday to Saturday evening.]

XIV,18. —... "You will fast for them (for the Jews) on Wednesday, for it is on *Wednesday* that they began to lose their souls and that they apprehended me. 19. The night which follows Tuesday belongs to Wednesday as it is written: It was evening and morning, one day; thus the evening belongs to the following day. 20. *Tuesday evening*, I ate my Pasch with you, and, during the night, they took me .... 21. And on Friday fast for them, because on that day they crucified me ...."

XIV,22-XVI,8. — [Fast and weep for the Jews, for this people has not believed in the Lord.] "For this reason pray and intercede for them, particularly on the days of the Pasch, so that, by your prayers, they may be judged

worthy of forgiveness and may turn towards our Lord
Jesus Christ.

XVII.—1. During the days of the Pasch, then, breth-
ren, you must pay special care and make your fast with the
greatest attention. Begin your fast when your brothers of
the (Jewish) people celebrate the Pasch, because, when
our Lord and Master ate the Pasch with us, he was delivered up by Judas after this hour and at once we began to
be afflicted because he was taken away from us. 2. Reckoning by the moon—we calculate as do the Hebrew faithful
—on the tenth day, a Monday, the priests and the ancients
of the people assembled and came into the fore-court of
Caiphas, the high priest. They took counsel how they
should arrest Jesus and put him to death, but they were
afraid and said: Not on a festival day, lest there be a
tumult among the people; for the whole world looked up
to him..." [Judas seeks an opportunity to betray Jesus]....

6. "Because of the crowds of all the (Jewish) people,
from every town and every village, who were coming up
to the Temple to celebrate the Pasch at Jerusalem, the
priests and the ancients took counsel, ordained and established that they would celebrate the feast immediately so
that they might arrest him without disturbance. The inhabitants of Jerusalem took part in the paschal sacrifice
and the meal and the people from outside the city had not
yet arrived; because they changed the days so that they
were reproved by God (who said to them): You are in all
things mistaken. 7. Thus they celebrated the Pasch three
days before its time, on the eleventh day of the moon,
Tuesday; for they said: The whole people has followed
him into error; now that we have the opportunity, we shall

arrest him, and when all the people have arrived we shall put him to death publicly so that the fact may be clearly known and all the people will turn away from him.

8. "Thus during the night which begins *Wednesday,* Judas delivered our Lord up to them. They had given him his reward on the tenth day of the moon, Monday. Hence God deals with them as if they had already taken him on the Monday, since it was on Monday that they conceived the plan of taking him and killing him; and it was on Friday that they carried out their evil (design), in accord with what Moses said of the Pasch: You shall keep it from the tenth to the fourteenth day and then all Israel shall sacrifice the Pasch."

XVII-XX,9. — [Fast, accordingly, during the days of the Pasch, beginning on Monday, and especially on Friday and Saturday; but be joyful on the day of the resurrection.] 10. "Observe the fourteenth day of the Pasch, wherever it falls, for the month and the day do not fall at the same time every year, but at different times. Hence, when this (Jewish) people celebrates the Pasch, you are to fast."

At first reading this chapter appears to be a compilation lacking any homogeneity. This characteristic has impressed the critics, not excepting Connolly who, while holding that one author is responsible for the *Didascalia,* nevertheless acknowledges "much confusion of thought and treatment in this chapter" (p. xxxii).

So, for example, the recommendation to observe the fourteenth day of the Pasch, wherever it may fall, whatever be the day and the month (XX,10), appears to contradict the principle of fasting from Monday to Saturday, which presupposes that the feast of the resurrection is fixed on a Sunday. This lack of coherence however might be explained by admitting that the Jewish Pasch served simply as an indication for determining the week in which the Christian Easter, fixed on a Sunday, was to fall.[8] It is always a delicate task to pick out the links between documents employed in a compilation, particularly when an editor has taken some pains to blend the documents and harmonize them. Nevertheless, there remain several repetitions and doublings concerning the fasts and the preparation for Easter.[9] Above all — and this is what interests us — there remain three statements, in different contexts, referring to the chronology of the passion.[10]

The first account (XIV,1-13) appears to constitute a unit, the ruling purpose of which is to justify the assertion of three days and three nights in the bowels of the earth; this is responsible for an unusual explanation of the darkness which descended on Friday. The three days of imprisonment have nothing to do with this explanation and were not, consequently, invented for the purposes of this argument. It does not even appear that, in the present form of the narrative, they have been manufactured so as to justify the Wednesday fast, for the structure of the account suggests rather an organic whole, originally independent, inserted by the author to justify the fasting law after its introduction.

The second passage (XIV,18-21) bears a different literary form, being contained in a discourse addressed by Jesus to his disciples. This time the Wednesday fast is brought into clear relation with the anniversary of Jesus' arrest. The text is attached rather loosely to a preceding exhortation which refers to a fast beginning on Monday. It is apparent that two different traditions have been combined and, since fasting through the whole of Passion Week is of later date than the original Wednesday and Friday fast (*Didache*, 8,1), the older of these two traditions must be the one which contains the three-day chronology of the passion.

The third account (XVII) appears to be a completely new development after the conclusion of the preceding paragraph.[11] It places the whole of the week of the passion in a different perspective, insisting this time on beginning the fast on Monday, the day on which the paschal lamb was chosen and on which Judas betrayed Jesus. To place the Supper on Tuesday evening has no longer any reason here; indeed it seems to embarrass the author considerably since he is obliged to invent an appropriate explanation, namely, that the priest and ancients of Jerusalem suddenly advanced the celebration of the Pasch so as to seize Jesus more easily! Clearly the author is here confronted with a chronology imposed on him by an earlier tradition. Everything would indicate that the editor of the chapter collected and combined different variations of a single tradition; or at least this is true of the first and second accounts.[12]

By itself, then, internal criticism of the chapter leads us to distinguish three accounts, of which the first two are the earliest and represent two aspects of the same theme. Consequently, the tradition of a Tuesday-evening Supper is *antecedent* to the composition of the *Didascalia*. In addition, this conclusion is confirmed by external witnesses, for this chapter of the *Didascalia* is by no means a completely isolated monument in the Christian tradition.

Let us consider first the case of *Epiphanius* who shares the opinion of the *Didascalia* on the date of the arrest of Jesus.[13]

Epiphanius was completely familiar with the *Didascalia* since he quotes it several times and speaks at length of the sect of the Audians who claimed to obey the directions of the *Didascalia* in the matter of celebrating Easter.[14] There are even details in Epiphanius which correspond exactly to those of the *Didascalia;*[15] and this proves, as Holl points out,[16] that Epiphanius read the *Didascalia* in a text which was, at the least, very close to our present text; but it also shows his dependence on this source.

Nevertheless in addition to the fact that Epiphanius adds to the *Didascalia* a certain number of personal details,[17] he does not in any fashion report the tradition of the *Didascalia* as a curious, an unusual, or even as a doubtful, explanation. He does not quote his source, but accepts as his own the chronology of the week of the passion, not only in his *Treatise on Heresies,* but also in the *De Fide:*

"Wednesday and Friday are days of fasting up to the ninth hour because, as Wednesday began, the Lord was arrested and on Friday he was crucified."[18]

At the same time Epiphanius knows the tradition of a Supper on Holy Thursday, for he refers, in the same passage of *De Fide,* to a ritual celebrated "in certain places" at the ninth hour of Thursday in Passion Week.[19] He also knows of a *modified* tradition, for, he says, certain people

relate that, on this Thursday, towards the ninth hour, the Apostles were able to meet secretly with Jesus and he performed the breaking of the bread with them in his prision."[20]

77

Yet Epiphanius is strong in his protests against the idea that the arrest was made during the night between Thursday and Friday.[21] For Epiphanius, accordingly, it is the tradition of a Thursday-evening Supper which is false; the certain tradition is that of Tuesday evening.

This conclusion is an important one and forbids our considering the testimony of Epiphanius as a simple repetition of the *Didascalia*. It is not that any great confidence may be placed in the critical sense of Epiphanius, which appears very slight; but it is just this fact which constitutes a rare piece of good fortune. He holds tenaciously to a tradition which he no longer understands. His Palestinian origins and his vast store of information are well known. If he maintains the Wednesday date it is because it was the most assured in the Oriental circle in which he lived. His source is certainly not purely a literary one.

The tradition that Jesus was arrested on Wednesday is found also in another author in whom no trace of the influence of the *Didascalia* is to be found, *Victorinus, bishop of Poetovio in Pannonia,* who died in 304.[22] In his little treatise, *De fabrica mundi,* Victorinus speaks of the days of creation and makes much of the fourth day (Wednesday) when the lights which regulate the course of the seasons were created. This number four possesses remarkable characteristics: the four elements, the four seasons, the four animals, the four Gospels, the four rivers of paradise, and, to close the list:

> "the man Jesus Christ, the author of all these things just mentioned, was *arrested* by evil-doers *on the fourth day*. We make the fourth day a day of fast by reason of his imprisonment, by reason of the majesty of his works, and so

that the course of the seasons may bring health to men, abundance to the harvests and calm to the inclemency of the weather."[23]

Victorinus also knows the fasts of Friday and Saturday, but he speaks of them without any reference to the interpretations of the *Didascalia*. The imprisonment of Jesus on Wednesday, the day of the number four, came to him by way of an absolutely *independent tradition* in a totally different context.

We are thus obliged to go back to a tradition common to both Victorinus and the *Didascalia*, one which is, accordingly antecedent to both. If we assign the *Didascalia* to the beginning of the third century, this tradition must have existed *in the course of the second century*. And so we encounter once again the results of internal criticism.

To these witnesses must be added the testimony of the *Book of Adam and Eve*. It is to be found in a passage which has already held our attention: the place which speaks of the sacrifice on the 92nd day, which foreshadows that of Calvary.

God accepted the sacrifice, and Adam said to Eve:

"Let us do this three times a week, throughout our life, on Wednesday, Friday and Sunday.[24] Then the Word of God said to Adam: Adam, you have determined in advance the days when *sufferings will come upon me* when I shall have become flesh; for those days are *Wednesday* and *Friday*. As for *Sunday*, that was the day on which I created all things and raised up the heavens. And by being *raised up* on that day I shall create joyfulness anew and I shall raise up those who believe in me. Adam, offer this sacrifice throughout all the days of your life....And Adam continued to offer this sacrifice, three times a week, until the end of the seven weeks. And on the first day (Sunday) which is the fiftieth day, Adam made an offering according to his custom."[25]

There does not appear to be any possibility of explaining the mention of sufferings on Wednesday, without calling upon the tradition that the passion began on Wednesday. As far as literary forms go, this work is completely independent of both the *Didascalia* and Victorinus of Pettau. Given the internal characteristics of the *Book of Adam and Eve* and of the *Didascalia,* if a common intellectual climate is to be sought for the two, then it would be a *Judaeo-Christian* one.

CHAPTER II

EARLY CHARACTER OF
THIS TRADITION

BEFORE the discovery of the old priestly calendar with its obligatory celebration of the Pasch on Tuesday evening, the various documents considered in the last chapter could only arouse astonishment. The most intelligent solution was undoubtedly that of Holl who realized that the Wednesday fast was linked with the arrest of Jesus. He went on to suggest that the Wednesday arrest had been invented in order to justify the primitive observance of the Wednesday fast. Such a solution, however, assumes that there was no firm, primitive tradition on the chronology of the passion. For it is impossible to see how anyone, simply in order to impose on the facts a harmony of very secondary importance, could have invented the inextricable difficulty of transposing the paschal meal of Jesus to three days before the Pasch.

The discovery of the fixed-day calendar resolves the problem. Purely from the point of view of textual criticism, it is possible to state that this tradition can go back only to a Chistian environment which was Jewish in its origins. We now know that the Jewish group whose influence was decisive in the formation of the Christian liturgy celebrated the Pasch on Wednesday. We are even obliged to say — on the supposition that there existed no solid tradition on the passion — that the first Judaeo-Christians would have been bound to fix the paschal meal of Jesus on Tuesday evening. The problem must now be formulated as follows. If such a tradition did not exist, they would have had to invent it. Did they project onto the life of Jesus the rhythm of their own liturgical life? Did they, in the manner so much favored by the priestly documents and by *Jubilees,* adapt the chronology of the passion to their concept of sacred history?

It must be admitted, should this hypothesis be correct, that the process of reshaping history was a rapid one, for the practice of celebrating Easter on Wednesday must have been superseded at an early date by the Sunday celebration. This would imply that the young community was in possession of a singularly facile creative ability with respect to contemporary events. In the last analysis, however, it is only by reference to the earliest accounts which we have of the passion that we can solve the question.

There is also another problem to be faced. To what extent did there exist in early Christianity a rival tradition of Thursday evening? Leaving aside for the moment the Gospels, we shall attempt to discover the moment when there appeared in the early Church a tradition placing the Supper *on the eve* of the death of Jesus.

The first allusion to the Supper occurs in St. Paul:

> "The Lord Jesus, the same night in which he was betrayed, (*en tē nukti hē paredideto*), took bread, and giving thanks, broke, and said..." (I Cor., 11,23-24).

The night in which he was betrayed, this is the earliest description of the night of the Supper. *The phrase is not*: "on the eve of his death." Attention is fixed on the arrest and, no doubt, also on the betrayal. It was this primitive formula which was to be adopted by the earliest liturgy in our possession.

Apostolic Tradition of Hippolytus:

> "Thy son...who, when he was being *delivered up* to a passion that he willed...taking bread, gave thanks and said..."[1]

Testament of our Lord Jesus Christ:

> "When he was being *delivered up* to a passion that he willed."[2]

Apostolic Constitutions:

> "The night in which he was *delivered up*" (VIII, 12).

83

These are the early formulas of the liturgy. The formula, "on the eve of his death," does not occur, to my knowledge, in any early liturgy, though it would have been the normal formula if the liturgy had followed a Thursday tradition. The Roman liturgy has preserved: *pridie quam pateretur,* on the eve of his *passion* (not of his death). An annual celebration of Holy Thursday finds no evidence before the second half of the fourth century.[3] The testimony of Epiphanius, which we have already seen, is a good indication of the period in which this annual festival was introduced.

We must take into account, also, in spite of its late date, the valuable source provided by the *Pilgrimage* of Etheria. The pilgrim describes the ceremonies of Holy Week at Jerusalem around the year 400.[4] The commemoration of the agony and death of Jesus is held on the Mt. of Olives and at Gethsemani during the night of Thursday to Friday.[5] Two points, however, should be noted. The sacrifice in the evening of Holy Thusday at which all communicated is celebrated at Golgotha, "behind the cross," an indication that tradition did not require any pilgrimage that evening to the place where Jesus had instituted the Eucharist. On the other hand, the first three days of Holy Week (Monday, Tuesday and Wednesday) are passed at the *Anastasis* (the Holy Sepulchre), but on Tuesday evening, after the dismissal, all go to the Mt. of Olives; after readings, prayer and Mass, the pilgrims return from there late in the night.[6] The ceremony evokes Jesus' teachings to his disciples "in the cave where the Lord used to instruct them." There is no reference to the agony of Jesus. This pilgrimage on *Tuesday evening,* however, might well be an ancient survival.[7]

It is only at a *very late date,* consequently, that *liturgical*

84

sources give evidence of a tradition placing the Supper on the eve of the death of Jesus. *Ecclesiastical writers,* on the contrary, supply allusions at least, from the *second half of the second century*.

In a chapter of the *Adversus Haereses,* preserved in a Latin translation, St. Irenaeus wishes to prove that Jesus' ministry lasted more than a year, since St. John's Gospel speaks of three Paschs. The text on the third Pasch is as follows:

> "It is written that six days before the Pasch, (Jesus) came to Bethany, that he went up from Bethany to Jerusalem, that he ate the Pasch and suffered *on the following day*" (*manducans pascha et sequenti die passus*).[8]

Evidently, for Irenaeus, this passing reference is the completely natural commentary on the Gospel text. It was not, therefore, such as to provoke discussion in the environment in which he lived. It is, however, to be noted — even if the formula, "the following day," is earlier than Irenaeus — that we have to do here with nothing more than an interpretation of the Gospel.

A difference of opinion among exegetes was likewise the occasion giving rise to the following pieces of evidence, the first of which is certainly earlier than Irenaeus. It is a frag.-ment of a work on Easter, preserved in the *Chronicon paschale,* and going back to Apollinaris, bishop of Hierapolis, in Phrygia, towards the year 165. Certain people, he notes, provoke disputes concerning Easter

> "because of their ignorance. They say that on the 14th day the Lord ate the lamb with his disciples and that he suf-

fered on the great day of Unleavened Bread. They claim
that Matthew speaks in this fashion. But this opinion is
opposed to the law and introduces a contradiction into
the Gospels."[9]

For the adversaries of Apollinaris, we may conclude from this,
Jesus celebrated his Supper the day before he died. Apollinaris
rejects the notion of crucifixion on 15 Nisan, the day of the
Pasch, stressing the difficulties implied in such a proposal; but
he does not tell us how he personally resolves the exegetical
debate.[10] In a second fragment, he states that

"on the true Pasch, the 14th day, it was the Son of God
who replaced the lamb."[11]

In the lack of any more precise statement on his part, it is most
probable that Apollinaris placed the Supper on 13 Nisan.

Clement of Alexandria, likewise, in a fragment also preserved in the *Chronicon paschale,* says:

"In the preceding years, the Lord ate the Pasch sacrificed
by the Jews and celebrated their festival. But when his
preaching was concluded, he who was the Pasch, the
Lamb of God, led like a sheep to the slaughter, instructed
his disciples in the mystery of this symbolism; this was on
that 13th day when they asked him: Where do you wish
us to prepare the Pasch? On this day, therefore, (......)
the sanctification of the unleavened bread and the preparation for the feast were carried out.... Our Lord suffered
the following day, he who was the Pasch offered by the
Jews .... Consequently on 14 when he suffered, the rulers

86

of the people and the scribes, having led him to Pilate,
would not enter the pretorium so as not to be defiled, for
they wished to eat the Pasch that evening without impedi-
ment. On this precise disposition (*akribeia*) concerning
the days all the Scriptures and the Gospels are agreed."[12]

"This precise statement concerning the days" on which
the whole tradition "is agreed" indicates evidently that Jesus,
the new Pasch, died at the moment when the paschal lamb
was sacrificed, on 14 Nisan.[13] This is the first statement. The
date of the Supper depends on the the death of Jesus, since
it is not disputed that it took place on the day before he died.

This text of Clement is of great interest because it places
the problem of the date of Jesus' death in precisely the terms
adopted by later exegesis. Now, since Clement, on his own
testimony, is inspired by a lost work, Melito of Sardes on
Easter,[14] from the same epoch as the work of Apollinaris,[15] it
is towards 165 that there is first found evidence of the difficulties encountered in reconciling the Johannine and the
Synoptic narratives.

Apart from this, the texts are silent. There is nothing in
the apostolic Fathers, nothing in Justin on the institution of
the Eucharist.[16] A phrase of the latter, however, must receive
our attention. It concerns the identification of Christ with the
Pasch. Justin addresses the Jews:

"The Pasch was the Christ, as Isaias says: Like a lamb he
was led to the slaughter. It was on the day of the Pasch
that you apprehended him, and it was also at the Pasch
that you crucified him; this is written."[17]

Justin distinguishes two phases in the symbolism of the Pasch

87

applied to Jesus: his arrest on the day of the Pasch and similarly, likewise (*oyoíōs*), his crucifixion during the Pasch. This text is easily explained on the supposition that Jesus celebrated the Pasch three days before the official Pasch; but this solution is by no means the only one possible.

Considering, therefore, only patristic writings, evidence for a Thursday evening Supper appears towards 165, but exclusively in the context of an exegetical debate arising out of the difficulties of harmonizing the Gospels. It is clearly a question of *deduction, not of tradition*.

As for the liturgy, it is perfectly logical with itself. It "remembers" only the Wednesday tradition. It preserves the original Wednesday fast in memory *of her Spouse's being taken away*:

"The days shall come when the Spouse will be taken away; in *those days* they shall fast."

In this fashion the *Didascalia* (Nau ed., p. 165) cites Matt., 9,15. Mark, 2,20 has the singular in the main manuscript tradition: "they shall fast *in that day*." But in the variants of Mark, in certain manuscripts of Matthew (D [Codex Bezae] it [most old Latin translations]), and in Lk., 5,35, the plural appears. Thus, with reference to the fast days prescribed by the *Didache*, Wednesday and Friday, we could find in a part of the *Gospel tradition* itself the statement that the Wednesday and Friday fasts are connected with the taking away of the Spouse. This is precisely the interpretation of the ancient patristic tradition. Tertullian certainly appears to link the Wednesday and Friday fasts to the taking away of the Spouse (*De jej.* 2; 14; cf. 13). The *Didascalia*, Epiphanius and Victorinus of Pettau are more precise about the significance of the Wednesday fast: it is the night when the Spouse was taken away, the night when Jesus was delivered up, that is, betrayed and arrested.

But, according as the memory of the three-day chronology was lost, it became necessary to reinterpret the liturgical tradition. On Wednesday Jesus had been *delivered up*. In the canon of the liturgies these words preserved all the force which they had had in *St. Paul*:

"the night in which he was betrayed."

But already in Peter of Alexandria (d. 311) the expression takes on a different sense:

"No one will blame us when we observe the fast of Wednesday and Friday on which tradition justly directs us to fast. Wednesday was the day on which the Jews *plotted* to have the Lord *delivered up* to them. Friday was the day on which he suffered for us."[18]

Thus Wednesday is still understood as the day on which Jesus was delivered up; but now he is delivered by the moral betrayal of Judas, not by the actual betrayal of the arrest.

A similar turn is given to the tradition in the *Apostolic Constitutions,* which is recognized to be a compilation. In *Const. Apost.,* V,15 (Funk ed., V,14, 20) the following statement is made without comment:

"He has directed us to fast on Wednesday and Friday, the first day because of his betrayal, the second because of his passion."

89

The Date of the Last Supper

A passage in VII,23, retains the memory of a "judgment (*krisis*) brought against the Lord" on Wednesday, but a gloss informs us that this "judgment" is that which was brought when Judas "promised" to deliver him. Chapter V,14 is curious in the extreme. In it is reconstructed a complete chronology of Holy Week in which Monday and Tuesday are taken up with the plotting of the Jews against Jesus, and Wednesday with the decision to put him to death. The editor is then led to distinguish *two* meals of Jesus. In one is foretold the betrayal by Judas ("one of you will betray me"); in the present structure of the account, this appears to be placed on Wednesday evening. The other is clearly placed on Thursday evening, and during it, Christ eats the Pasch and institutes the Eucharist. This bizarre solution is evidently the sign of vagueness in the tradition on the last meal of Jesus.

The *Didascalia of Addai* interprets differently the original connection between Wednesday and the passion. On that day Jesus made "revelations" concerning his sufferings and death.[19] The *Book of Adam and Eve,* on the contrary, maintained firmly the original connection.

Having reached this point in our research, we may state that the results obtained by study of patristic writings confirm those of the calendar. The sole likely date for the paschal meal was, according to liturgical analogy, the Wednesday. The earliest Christian tradition, that which is rooted in the primitive Judaeo-Christian community, gives evidence pointing in the same direction.[20] It is the only tradition which can be primitive — for *there is no tradition concerning Thursday evening*. The Wednesday tradition marked the liturgy with an indelible imprint, imposing on it the Wednesday fast. It has nothing about it indicative of an eccentric or lateral

90

tradition. It is not the expression of the opinion of a peripherical group. It blends with the central axis of the Christian liturgy.

Faced with such evidence, we finally come to the essential question. Are the Gospel narratives opposed to the liturgical tradition?

Third Part

The Gospels

CHAPTER I

SOLUTION OF THE CONFLICT
BETWEEN JOHN AND THE SYNOPTICS

EVER since Christian reflection began to compare the Gospels among themselves — that is, as we have seen, since the second half of the second century — the conflict between the Johannine and the Synoptic traditions concerning *the day of Jesus' death* has made itself felt. The elements of the problem have become classic.[1] The Synoptics present the last meal of Jesus as a *paschal meal* (Mk., 14,12-16; Matt., 26,17-19; Lk., 22,7-15). If, then, the Synoptics followed the official Jewish calendar, Jesus would have eaten the Pasch on 14 Nisan in the evening, and would have been crucified on 15

Nisan. This solution has never, in fact, completely satisfied exegetes, for it is difficult to admit so much activity on the part of the Jews during the night and day of the Pasch which were sacred and times of rest. On the contrary, according to John, when the Jews brought Jesus to Pilate, they had *not yet* eaten the Pasch, since they refused to enter the pretorium

> "that they might not be defiled, but that they might eat the Pasch" (Jn., 18,28).

Jesus dies on 14 Nisan during the immolation of the lambs in the Temple (cf. Jn. 19,36).

> "It was the eve of the Pasch" (Jn., 19,14).

Faced with this apparent inconsistency, certain critics have adopted an attitude of radical skepticism, denying all historicity to any chronology of the passion.[2] Others have proposed various attempts at reconciliation. The most interesting is certainly that which places Jesus' death on 14 Nisan, and suggests that he anticipated the date of the paschal meal. But how was it possible to *anticipate* this meal? The hypothesis of a divergence of calendar has been proposed. In particular, it has been suggested that there was a difference of one day in the calculation of the new moon, a difference which could have divided Judeans and Galileans; but this hypothesis has never been able to find solid support. Others have denied the paschal character of the Last Supper. The proximity of Jesus' last meal to the Pasch would have encouraged the attribution of a paschal significance to it, theological reasons supplying a motive. But this solution compromises the historical character of the very clear statement of the Synoptics.

If, however, one applies to the Gospel narratives the tradition preserved in the first account of the *Didascalia,* the contrast between John and the Synoptics disappears of itself. The chronology is then the following:

Jesus celebrates the Pasch *on Tuesday evening, the eve of the Pasch,* according to the *old* priestly calendar.

He is arrested in the night between Tuesday and Wednesday.

He dies on *Friday,* 14 *Nisan,* the *eve of the Pasch,* according to the *official* calendar.

The old Pasch and the official Pasch would accordingly, have been celebrated that year at a distance of three days from one another. This could have been by chance. But this rather feeble evasion leads one to adopt the hypothesis of a modified calendar, proposed above as being very probable in the Jewish circle which gave birth to Christianity. The choice of the Wednesday which preceded the official Pasch made it possible for the full moon to fall *within the seven days of the paschal festival,* calculated according to the old priestly calendar.

According to this explanation, then, *the Synoptic Gospels* preserved a primitive tradition corresponding to a Palestinian catechesis. In such a context the Pasch celebrated by Jesus could only be that of the old calendar. Explanations were, therefore, superfluous.

In Mk., 14,12 (cf. Lk., 22,7) the text runs:

> "On the first day of the unleavened bread, when they sacrificed the Pasch."

The explanatory phrase, "when they sacrificed the Pasch," which does not appear in the text of Matt., seems to be a secondary gloss, intended to show that this first day of the

97

unleavened bread[3] was the day in the evening of which the festival of the unleavened bread began. This means that it was the eve of the Pasch (which eliminates the hypothesis of 13 Nisan). It is also possible that the glossator, who was so concerned to stress that it was the eve of the Pasch, no longer knew which Pasch was in question. This gloss leaves untouched the problem of knowing whether or not Jesus ate the paschal lamb at the Supper.[4]

The fourth Gospel was certainly prepared with a different object in view and with an eye to a Hellenistic climate of thought. It is probable that, in the diaspora, the only Pasch was that of the 15th day of the lunar month. The note preserved by Al-Biruni on the Magarya states that their paschal observances were obligatory only for those who lived in Israel. From another point of view, there runs through the whole of St. John's Gospel that theological preoccupation which already betrays itself in the prologue in the antithetical parallelism, Jesus-Moses. Worship in the Spirit, initiated by Jesus, has replaced the rites and celebrations of legalistic Judaism.[5] Thus the activity of Jesus is presented as moving to the rhythm of the official Jewish feasts, feasts to which he alone brings fulfilment.[6] At the final Pasch, he is the paschal lamb who supplants all the sacrifices of the Temple. In such a perspective, it is the festivals of official Judaism which hold interest for the Johannine tradition. Dates are based on the official Pasch. It is "before the festival day of the Pasch" (Jn., 13,1) — and not on the eve — that the washing of the feet and the farewell discourse take place, while Pilate's judgment is given *"on the eve* of the Pasch" (Jn., 19,14).[7]

The two points of view, that of the Synoptics and that of John, are thus basically different. The two traditions do not speak of the same Pasch. These considerations could explain in part the silence of the Synoptics regarding the official Jewish feasts. They throw considerable light on the *later Easter disputes*.[8] A liturgical tradition in the line of the Palestinian catechesis preserved in the Synoptics had no reason to celebrate Easter on the official, movable day, but rather according to the day of the week. The Roman liturgy, based on a catechesis similar to that of Mark, was of this kind. When he defended — if with too unbending a rigor — the Sunday Easter, Pope Victor was indeed following, as he asserted, an apostolic tradition (*H.E.* V, 23,1; 24,9-10).

But the people of Asia were no less faithful to a Johannine tradition! St. John's Gospel makes no mention of any Pasch but that of 14 Nisan, the official feast of the Jews. It was quite normal that, for them, the only anniversary of the Pasch was 14 Nisan, the day of the crucifixion. They "kept the 14th day of the Pasch, *in accordance with the Gospel*" and following John and Polycarp (*H.E.* V, 24,3-6). This does not exclude the possibility of earlier discussions and disputes concerning the calendar. There must have existed a certain freedom in Asia Minor. Pontus and Osroene were in agreement with Rome, not with Ephesus (*H.E.* V, 23,3-4). Easter disputes are mentioned in Phrygia towards 165.[9] Questions concerning the calendar seem always to have been the order of the day in these countries. Whom had St. Paul in mind, then, when he, the former Pharisee, attached by tradition to the lunar calendar, denounced those who remained slaves to the law by observing

"the days, the months, the seasons and the years" (Gal., 4,10; cf. Col., 2,16; Rom., 14,5)?

The difference in points of view existing between the Synoptics and St. John also accounts for a detail, though this time a minor one, in their chronologies. This concerns the date of the *anointing at Bethany*. According to Jn., 12,1, the meal at Bethany is placed six days before the Pasch (*pro hex hēmerōn tou pascha*), whereas in the tradition of Mk./Matt. the meal occurs just after it has been noted that the Pasch was to take place "after two days" (Matt., 26,2; Mk., 14,1).[10] There is a difficulty here which has generally been solved by saying that Mk./Matt. have "transferred" the anointing into the context of the passion. If, however, John is speaking of the official Pasch and Mk./Matt. of the old Pasch, the difficulty is removed, or at least markedly simplified.

By counting back six days from the legal Pasch, that is from Friday evening, exclusive, we come to Saturday evening for the anointing at Bethany, according to John's account.[11] By counting back two days from the old Pasch, that is, from Tuesday evening, exclusive, we come to Sunday evening, or to Saturday evening, depending on the sense given the expression: *meta duo hēmeras*.[12] It seems clear that one should not press to closely the phrase:

> "the feast of the Pasch and of the Azymes was after two days."

According to the same Mk./Matt. tradition, the first day of Azymes began on Tuesday morning, which shortens the time between the anointing and Azymes. The impression to be gained is of a certain concomitance between the anointing, the acclamation of Jesus and the assembly of the chief priests in Mk./Matt. Hence harmonization with John no longer requires that the episode be transferred.

It should be noted also that the tradition of Mark has preserved the memory of *two days* following upon the entry of Jesus into Jesusalem on the day of palms (Mk., 11,12-20). Now this day is placed by John on the day after the anointing at Bethany, thus on the Sunday (Jn., 12,12), whereas the Synoptic catechesis, which has Jesus going up only once to Jerusalem, places it in a quite different literary context, well before the account of the passion (Mk., 11,1-10 and par.). Here the implicit harmony with John is highly interesting, for, in the new explanation, only two mornings can intervene in the Synoptic tradition between Palm Sunday and the arrest. Mark *alone* has preserved the memory of these two mornings.[13]

Without falling prey to the superstition of strict concordance, we may propose the following as a possible chronology for the days preceding the Supper:

Saturday evening: anointing at Bethany (Jn., 12,1-8; Matt., 26,6-13; Mk., 14,3-9).

"The following day" (Jn., 12,12), *Sunday*, Solemn entry of Jesus (Matt., 21,1-9; Mk., 11,1-10; Lk., 19,28-38).

Jesus returns to sleep at Bethany (Mk., 11,11; Matt., 21,17).

"The following day" (Mk., 11,12), *Monday*: Jesus leaves Bethany and curses the fig-tree.

"The following morning" (Mk., 11,20), *Tuesday*: The disciples notice the dried-up fig-tree. They ask where the Pasch should be prepared (Mk., 14,12 and par.).

"In the evening" Jesus sits down at table with his disciples (Mk., 14,17 and par.).[14]

101

CHAPTER II

THE EVENTS OF THE PASSION
IN THE CHRONOLOGY OF THREE DAYS

THE chronology which we have suggested eliminates the conflict between John and the Synoptics. But a difficulty still remains. The Gospels do not appear to have kept any memory of the three days of the passion. This must be examined more closely.

Considering only the content of the Gospel narratives, taken as a whole, one question arises demanding an answer. If Jesus was arrested the day before the crucifixion, how could *so many events* take place in the space of time between the arrest and the crucifixion? Let us confine ourselves for the moment to the Synoptic account.

Jesus is lead before the high priest.

"*all* the priests and the scribes and the ancients assembled together (*sunerchontai*)" (Mk., 14,53), "*all* the council" Mk., 14,55).

Witnesses are sought

"and they found none" (Mk., 14,55);

nevertheless, several depositions are made, but they are contradictory (Mk., 14,56); only *later* (*husteron*), (Matt., 26,60) do witnesses present themselves to accuse Jesus of wishing to destroy the Temple (Mk., 14,56-58; Matt., 26,60-61). It is then that the high priest makes his solemn adjuration and the unanimous judgment is heard: He deserves to die.

The impression emerging from these accounts is not that of a precipitous judgment. If the evidence of St. Mark is accepted, the session of the Sanhedrin cannot be reduced to a hasty meeting of a handful of members in the middle of the night, nor to the hearing of two or three witnesses hired in advance. The Sanhedrin has assembled in due form;[1] witnesses have to be found. Could all of this have possibly taken place in the few hours at the end of the night?

Mk./Matt. insert after this the scene of the mocking (which Luke places earlier), then a *second* session of the Sanhedrin "early in the morning." Once again, the Sanhedrin assembles in its entirety (Mk., 15,1). This time there is no delay, and Jesus is taken to Pilate (Mk., 15,1 and par.).

Was the governor likely to appear on summons in order to try a miscreant? He had not the same reasons for haste as the priests. The texts indicate that he hesitates; he questions Jesus several times, being embarrassed by this unusual case (Mk., 15,2-5; Matt., 27,11-14). Learning that Jesus is a Galilean, he sends him to Herod (Lk., 23, 6-12). The episode with Herod, reported by Luke alone, has been considered legendary. While in itself it is not at all an unlikely occurrence, yet it must be admitted that it is difficult to find a place for this extra event — with all the circumstances reported by Luke[2] — in the already crowded lines of our time-table.

In any event, Luke distinguishes *two appearances* before Pilate. For the second of these, Pilate has *summoned* (*sugkalesamenos*) the principal priests and leaders of the people (Lk., 23,13; cf. Matt., 27,17) who, it would appear from this, had dispersed. Matthew, too, suggests an interval, since he inserts here the episode of Judas' remorse and his visit to the priests and elders (Matt., 27,3 f.). Even in this second session, the sentence is not passed immediately. Pilate discusses the matter with the crowd and, for the sake of peace, finally releases Barabbas (Matt., 27,15-26; Mk., 15,6-15; Lk., 23,13-28). To all this must be added the scourging and the preparations for the execution.

It might also be considered that, for all the fickleness of public opinion, the account acquires greater credibility if the priests are given at least a full day to work on the people and win them to their side.

Admittedly, up to the present, Christian tradition as a whole has considered that all the events of Jesus' passion took place during what remained of a single night and the next morning; but it must be acknowledged that such a telescoping of events is hardly satisfactory for the inquiring mind. As well, this solution is tenable only at the price of "inter-

preting" the text in Mark which shows Jesus *on the cross* at
9 o'clock in the morning ("it was the third hour when they
crucified him," Mk., 15,25). The attempt has been made to
lengthen the morning by bringing this "third hour" up to the
time mentioned by John for Pilate's *judgment,* that is, mid-day
("it was about the sixth hour," Jn., 19,14). The longer time-
table of John is thus preferred to the shorter one of Mark.

Now, Mark's figure — crucifixion at the third hour — is
precisely the one adopted by the liturgical tradition.[3] Consequently, the suggestion has been made that Mark divides
time into three-hour periods and that this is a liturgical, not
an historical, division. But the question one should rather ask
is whether the liturgical tradition is not, perhaps, the older
and better substantiated one.[4] The *Didascalia* also says that
Jesus remained six hours on the cross. It is curious to
notice that, to the degree that the three-day chronology is lost,
the time of the crucifixion is modified. For it was necessary to
prolong the Friday morning. The *Apostolic Constitutions* re-
versed the times in the most logical fashion. At the third hour
Pilate's sentence, at the sixth hour the crucifixion (V,14;
VIII,34). Epiphanius, who places the Supper on Tuesday evening likewise maintains the third hour, basing himself on
Mark *and on John.* He asserts that "certain copies" of St.
John's Gospel have altered the sign which stand for the figure
3 (gamma) into the sign standing for the figure 6 (zeta), as a
result of a slight scribal error. This was known, he states, to
Clement, Origen and Eusebius Pamphilius.[5] It is true that the
present manuscript variants on the times in John and Mark are
not of great assistance to us and that, up to the present,
nothing clear has been discovered in Clement and Origen.[6]
But Eusebius of Caesarea, at least, confirms Epiphanius in a

text preserved both in a Greek chain and in a Syriac letter of Severus of Antioch.[7] In addition, the testimony of Epiphanius is corroborated by a fragment of the *Chronicon paschale* claiming the support of an Ephesian tradition.[8]

Whatever be the truth of the matter, and even if John's doubtful figure be allowed, the space of time is very short and it is extremely difficult to imagine how so many events were compressed into so few hours.[9] In any event, to appeal to St. John's Gospel only heightens the difficulty of the horary, for it means adding to the Synoptic list the appearance before Annas and the high priest's questioning (Jn., 18,13-24).

This raises another question which has always greatly perplexed exegetes. *How do the events* reported by the different evangelists *fit into one another?*

There is a contradiction between the tradition of Mk./ Matt. and that of Luke concerning the time of the trial. In all four Gospels the three-fold denial takes place during the night following the arrest; but Mk./Matt. insert the trial before the high priest *into the context* of the Peter episode (Matt., 26,58-75; Mk., 14,54-72). If, then, the denials occurred during the night, it necessarily follows that the trial was also held at night. Yet in Luke, the trial, the only one reported, is held during the day (Lk., 22,66). John supports Luke; with him the night of the arrest is occupied by the questioning by Annas, the high priest. The matter has appeared so unreasonable that many critics suggest that, in Jn., 18,24 should be removed and inserted between v. 13 and v. 14 so as to have the denials and the interrogation take place in the house of Caiphas and not that of Annas. But this arbitrary transposition becomes altogether unnecessary if one follows the chronology of the first account of the *Didascalia*. According to this, it was during the day of Wednesday that Jesus was kept in the house of Caiphas and that the chief priests took counsel concerning him. The questioning to which Jesus was submitted is very different from the scene of the trial; there is, consequently, no reason for having it take place before Caiphas.

There is nothing new about this exegesis which refuses to see the nocturnal interrogation as the trial before the Sanhedrin. It is already to be found in the *Diatessaron* of Tatian who harmonized the Gospel accounts by placing the two last of Peter's denials at the moment when Jesus leaves the house of Annas to be led before Caiphas. Only *later* do the chief priests and the scribes hold their meeting.[10] This manner of arranging the events has been adopted once again by modern exegetes,[11] independently of the first account in the *Didascalia*, which, evidently, confims their interpretation.

But the *Didascalia* also affirms that Jesus was not led before Pilate until Thursday, and this solves the problem of the second session of the Sanhedrin "in the morning, early," reported by Mk./Matt. The first session, a long one, took place on Wednesday, the second on Thursday morning.

It is now possible to understand how the Mk./Matt. tradition grew up. The memory of Peter's denial in the house of the high priest had been preserved. Now, Mark and Matthew mention only one high priest.[12] Consequently, they placed Peter's denial in the house of Caiphas. What is more serious, this foreshortening of perspective led the Mk./Matt. tradition to report *only one* session during which *the high priest questioned Jesus*. And, since the principal session was the trial, it has been transported to the same place as the interrogation by Annas, and so inserted in the episode of Peter's denial. It should be observed that this solution might well solve another problem, that of the *place* of trial, which is no longer necessarily the palace of Caiphas.[13]

But, *why should there be two sessions of the Sanhedrin,* separated by only one day? The reply is given in a text of the Mishna which regulates as follows the Jewish procedure in capital cases:

> "In non-capital cases the trial takes place during the day, and the verdict may be delivered during the night. In capital cases the *trial* takes place *during the day*, and the verdict must also be delivered *during the day*. In non-capital cases the verdict of acquittal or condemnation may be delivered the same day; in capital cases a verdict of acquittal may be delivered the same day, but *a verdict of condemnation may not be delivered until the following day*. For this reason, no trials may be held *on the eve of a sabbath* or *on the eve of a festival*" (Sanh., 4,1).

Faced with the evidence of this text — which is at variance with the normally accepted chronology — certain authors have expressed doubt as to whether these laws were applied in the time of Jesus. The Mishna, however, contains a very ancient form of Jewish law and the presumption is in its favor. In addition, these prescriptions are quite logical, for a nocturnal process has little chance of being legal in any civilized country; and the like is to be said for a trial carried through in a single day without any preliminary enquiry. For these reasons, it has been more usual to maintain that the Jewish authorities pushed rapidly through Jesus' trial on the plea that only the Romans could pass the death sentence and that they were thus dispensed from applying their own Jewish rules of procedure. This opinion will, clearly, have to be re-examined.

The men who condemned Jesus, did so in the name of the law, accusing him of blasphemy, the gravest of crimes in their eyes. This obliged them to apply the laws themselves in their full integrity. It is entirely characteristic of the legalistic mind to observe juridical forms scrupulously, even when, in present circumstances, they no longer correspond to the purpose for which they were established. Moreover, to hand Jesus over to Pilate for condemnation to death was to accept responsibility for the verdict; this is the only way in which the religious authorities of the nation could have understood the action. In order to discredit totally in the eyes of the people the leader and the movement which was growing up around him, it was indispensable to safeguard the legal and the strictly Jewish character of the decisions taken. A condemnation ordered by the Romans had very little weight for these religious Jews who were ready to sacrifice their lives rather than incur a defilement contrary to the Law.[14] What was required was a verdict pronounced by the legitimate authorities, made in the name of the Law and in defense of the Law.[15]

It is a very striking fact that the rules laid down by the Mishna are in complete harmony with the *Didascalia* and, at the same time, correspond to the internal demands of the Gospel texts. Here we find justification for the two sessions of the Mk./Matt. tradition; the first, during the day (Lk., 22,66), with a prolonged hearing of witnesses — the trial session; the second, much more rapid, the following morning:

> "When morning was come, (they) took counsel against Jesus, that they might put him to death" (Matt., 27,1)

— the session when the verdict was delivered. By breaking up the sessions in this way, we find fresh light thrown upon the deliberations of the Sanhedrin which, to use a phrase of Fr. Vogt, have always been a conundrum.[16]

Furthermore, according to the Mishna, the chief priests and the scribes, if they desired an immediate trial, could not have had Jesus arrested during the night of Thursday to Friday, the eve of both the sabbath and the Pasch. On the other hand, an arrest during the night of Tuesday to Wednesday could have given hope for a solution by Thursday. Pilate's hesitations delayed things to Friday.

As regards another point also the three-day chronology satisfies the requirements of the Mishna and, in addition, eliminates an internal contradiction seen up to the present in the Mk./Matt. tradition. The priests and the scribes decided not to seize Jesus during the feast (Mk., 14,2; Matt., 26,5) — and immediately they arrest him, on the eve of the Pasch.[17]

The chronology of the first part of the passion may, accordingly, be established fairly easily, taking into account three traditions: Mk./Matt., Luke and John. These traditions present an episodic narrative with their complementary details and different "abridgements" which must be isolated in order to explain their mutual divergences. The events unfold in the following manner:

Night of Tuesday to Wednesday: Jesus arrested, brought to the house of the high priest (Mk., 14,53; Lk., 22,54), Annas (Jn., 18,13).

Questioning by high priest (Jn., 18,19-23).

Jesus brought to house of Caiphas (Jn., 18,19-23).

Day of Wednesday: trial session (Mk., 14,55-64 and par.) Jesus mocked.[18]

Thursday morning:[19] session for verdict (Matt., 27,1; Mk., 15,1).

Jesus is immediately brought before Pilate (Matt., 27,2; Mk., 15,1; Lk., 23,1; Jn., 18,28).

John adds at once:

"The Jews went not into the hall, that they might not be defiled, but that they might eat the Pasch" (Jn., 18,28).

But this does not necessarily bring us to Friday morning, as I formerly believed. For a tradition of the Mishna, glossed by the rabbis, notes that the defilement contracted by entering the house of a pagan lasted seven days; for, because of the risk that a foetus might be buried in the place, this defilement was equiparated with that contracted in the house of one who had died, in accordance with Num., 19,14. This prescription was valid only in Palestine.[20] Consequently, there is no longer any difficulty in placing the appearance before Pilate, as reported by John, on Thursday morning.[21]

John and Mark bring together as one the two appearances before Pilate, but Luke, with his report of the sending of Jesus to Herod and the new summoning of the chief priests, is very favorable to the hypothesis of two, consecutive days, Thursday and Friday. Matthew, too, is better explained in this fashion.[22] The events would thus be disposed as follows:

Day of Thursday: appearance before Pilate.

Sent to Herod (Lk., 23,6-12).

Friday morning: new appearance before Pilate (Lk., 23,13).

Condemnation. Crucifixion.

The events of the passion are thus distributed in a much more reasonable fashion over a period of two-and-a-half days than over the interval permitted if the Supper were on Thursday evening. The suggested chronology shows the implicit coherence of the Gospel narratives, which appears all the more clearly in the measure that greater respect is shown the literal sense of the texts. It thus resolves many of the objections raised against the historicity of the account.

Some exegetes, however, will continue to see a difficulty in the two-fold trial of Jesus.[23] This objection, as Mr. Goguel himself points out,[24] does not take sufficient account of the meagerness of our information concerning juridical procedure in Palestine at the time of the procurators. Nor does it weigh sufficiently the complexity and the flexibility of concrete facts, particularly in the case of Jesus.

Our suggested solution restores to the Jewish procedure, in harmony with the Synoptic tradition, a legal character which the critics have renounced. We have already indicated the reasons which made a trial carried out according to the Jewish legal forms appear psychologically and religiously necessary: Jesus must not appear as a martyr of the anti-Roman cause. The appeal to the Roman jurisdiction was probably obligatory — at least theoretically — in order to have a sentence of death ratified.[25] But, in the case of Jesus, a Roman trial was indispensable since he was accused of being an agitator who was raising the people up against Caesar.[26] The Jewish authorities wished to make sure of the cooperation of the Roman authorities. There are several possible reasons for that. They may have feared a popular rising in

113

support of Jesus (Mk., 14,2; Matt., 26,5). The division of the Jewish parties might have seemed favorable to a disturbance of order. They may have been alarmed at finding themselves compromised with the Roman government by a "messiah" in whom they did not believe and on whom the aspirations of the people were beginning to fix themselves (cf. Jn., 11,48). Finally, however paradoxical it may appear after the last two reasons, there was the possibility that Jesus might find support among those circles whose members maintained contact with the Romans. He ate with publicans; he had dealings with centurions (Matt., 8,5); pagans wished to see him (Jn., 12,20). Any possible sympathy had to be cut off by committing the Roman authority to active opposition to him.[27]

It remains to make clear how the explicit memory of the three days of the passion could have been lost in the present Gospel accounts.

The primitive catechesis was much more interested in the substance of events and in their doctrinal significance than in their chronological connection. It transmitted the *kerygma* of the message and developed the events which had bearing on this message. (Cf. the summaries of catechesis preserved in Acts 2,22-36; 10,36-43). It kept in mind the details of interest to it, but it was little concerned with dates. This indifference to the biographical aspect is very evident in St. Mark's Gospel which, nevertheless, is presented in the form of a narrative. It does not allow us either to place dates on the ministry of Jesus or to estimate its length. Foreshortenings, accordingly, were easily admitted. The *two* questionings before Annas and Caiphas, *both* of them high priests, could merge into one in Mk./Matt. The same is true of the *two* sessions of the Sanhedrin in Luke and the *two* appearances before Pilate in Mark and John. What was important was to make known the substance of the events of the passion, the appalling scandal of the crucified Messiah-King, the responsibility of those involved, whatever, in short, could present the Church's teaching to the new catechumens. The elimination of reduplicated elements was intended to simplify catechetical summaries. When this catechesis passed from a Palestinian environment to a pagan world, which knew only the Pasch of the Jews of the diaspora on the 15th day of the lunar month, it was inevitable that the Last Supper of Jesus should tend to be associated with the legal Pasch. The Gospel tradition solidified only slowly; for many years it remained relatively fluid, in close relationship with the oral catechesis.

The most obvious example is the transference by Mk./ Matt. of the principal session of the Sanhedrin to the preceding night. This undoubtedly presupposes that the true circumstances in which the trial took place had been forgotten and that eye-witnesses had disappeared. We must not forget the conditions under which the Christian message was transmitted in the Roman community. The height of the persecution of 64, under Nero, was not the moment to pay close attention to chronological details; what was important was to hand on the essential message of salvation. Nor was there any necessity to do great violence to a tradition already fixed in its substance. The passage, Mk., 14,55-65, forms a unit within Peter's denial. It could have been simply transposed from its original place (between 14,72 and 15,1). All that had to be done then was to retouch slightly v. 53b. But we shall never know the original text of the night interrogation in Mark.

If accepted, the new hypothesis would not be without

value for the history of the formation of the Gospels. For it provides a privileged opportunity for studying, from a known starting-point, the modifications which the three-day chronology has undergone in each tradition as it follows its own line of development. It would be normal for such an enquiry to corroborate the results already obtained by literary criticism of the texts.

We can observe how Matthew follows Mark in the transposition mentioned, and how he improves upon it in 26,57, where he adds the gloss, "Caiphas." This makes clear the secondary character of the present Greek Matthew with respect to Mark, something which has long been recognized by the critics. Yet, at the same time, the material which he employs — here observations already made will come to mind — is often earlier and more informed than that of Mark. There is the "later" of v. 60; the remark in 27,1 that the session had been called to put Jesus to death; the assembly summoned by Pilate in v. 17.

It is noteworthy that Luke, who makes careful use of Mark, has not followed him in the transposition of the night session. Doubtless, he possessed other information; yet it might also be suggested that he had to hand an earlier edition of Mark. Moreover, the author of the third Gospel, always more concerned than the others with the order of events, seems to have felt a certain embarrassment when faced with divergent traditions which he no longer understood. Having in his possession a tradition that Jesus appeared before Herod, he alone had to face the problem of time; he reduced to one the two sessions of the Sanhedrin.

As for St. John's treatment, it is altogether original, as is normal for this Gospel. John passes over the two sessions of the Sanhedrin, but by way of compensation he lingers over the questioning by Annas. One cannot avoid the impression that this was a matter of personal experience and recollection ("the other disciple," 18,5). He compresses into one the two appearances before Pilate, guided here by a theology of the kingship of Jesus. The literary and theological center of the episode, now considered as unique, is the crown of thorns.[28] Personal memories, theological development, these were the characteristics of John's Gospel. The three-day chronology shows that the basic information of the fourth Gospel corresponds, as far as dates are concerned, with that of the Synoptics, even though a completely different line of development has been followed.

Frequent attempts have been made to establish the laws governing the formation and transmission of the basic elements of the Gospels. As regards the accounts of the passion, the results of our analysis prove that the transmission of the Gospel obeyed the laws of *compression* and of *elimination of duplicated episodes*. This offers reassurance regarding fidelity to sources. Under the shield of their apostolic authority, the Church kept in mind episodes and accounts apparently contradictory and difficult to harmonize. Untroubled by any lack of coherence, she kept in the heart of her liturgy the tradition of Wednesday as the day on which her Spouse was taken away. The significance attached to this tradition evolved progressively, but she never consented to renounce either of the two ends of the chain, even when she no longer saw the links: *the Supper, a paschal meal; Jesus, the paschal lamb.*

CONCLUSION

IN conclusion, far from contradicting the liturgical tradition and the liturgical parallels, the Gospels confirm
them; and the harmony is all the more deep-seated because it
is not consciously sought. The chronology of the passion
which possesses the earliest authentication, because it is of
Judaeo-Christian origin, resolves the conflict between John
and the Synoptics concerning the day of Jesus' death. It makes
more intelligible the development of events in the various
accounts of the passion. The thesis that the Supper was held
on Tuesday evening, though it might appear revolutionary,
reveals itself in fact as eminently conservative.

This new solution permits closer contact with certain

aspects of the primitive Christian faith. For the first Christian generation, Jesus had celebrated the Pasch at the beginning of the night between Tuesday and Wednesday, following the sacred calendar which had imposed its rhythm on the march of the people in the desert and which regulated the ancient liturgy of the Temple. The Last Supper was thus charged with all the memories of the venerable priestly tradition. It took the place of the sacrificial meals of the Old Law. It was the culmination of the liturgy of unleavened bread. But by dying on Friday, the eve of the official Pasch, Jesus took the place of the lambs sacrificed in the Temple. He would henceforward be the unique victim, offered in place of lambs and goats. Summing up these two lines of sacrifice, Christ gathered together the two-fold heritage of the Jewish tradition and brought it to its fulfilment. There can be no doubt that this was the primitive belief of the Christian community: "Purge out the old leaven ... Christ our Pasch is sacrificed" (I Cor., 5,7).

These days spoke to the disciples of Jesus.

> "Why — asked Ben Sira — doth one day excel another ... ?
> By the knowledge of the Lord they were distinguished ....
> Some of them God made high and great days, and some
> of them he put in the number of ordinary days."[1]

They spoke with all their paschal symbolism. They spoke as days already consecrated by the old calendar. There can be no doubt that the existing celebration of these liturgical days guided Christian piety and contributed with all its authority to giving these days a position of importance in the week of the Passion.[2] The harmonies were, indeed, plain and clamoring for attention. God, the master of the times of history, as the *Book of Daniel* magnificently shows him, had himself governed the course of events, all of them obedient to his hand. On *Wednesday,* Jesus was delivered up; on *Friday,* he died. These days were signs of God; they spoke a language which was clear and intelligible to the first Christian community. The most holy of all histories, that of the Messiah who fulfilled the Scriptures, unfolded according to a consecrated ritual. Unique High Priest of the New Alliance, he "gave himself up willingly to death," knowing that "the hour" had come, "at the appointed time" (*kata kairon*). The final "sign" would be that of the *Sunday* of Resurrection, the first day of the liturgical week, the dawn of the new time, which — because it is the first and the eighth day — opened the great messianic week.[3]

Not the least astonishing of the consequences of the new system of dates are these profound harmonies which lead us into the heart of the primitive Christian liturgy. We have not completed our explorations of the varied aspects of the field which lies open to research, close to that of the documents of Qumran. There are questions concerning the interpretation of the priestly documents and the diversity of Jewish centers of thought at the time of Jesus and their relations with one another and with the Temple. There are questions, too, concerning the process of formation of the Gospels and the Palestinian origins of the Roman liturgy.

Perhaps it will one day be possible for us to understand better the dimensions of the drama which was played in Judea in the first century of our era. But here we are entering into another order of reality. This new chronology of the passion concerns the science of Christian origins. Yet it cannot be of indifference to the heart of a believer.

Appendices

APPENDIX I

THE DATE OF *JUBILEES* AND
THE FIGURE OF JUDA, SON OF JACOB

THE date of *Jubilees* has been the subject of considerable controversy. Indications on the history of the question and the criteria of dating will be found in the introduction of Charles to his edition of *Jubilees,* in Frey ("Apocryphes de l'Ancien Testament," *D. B. S.* I 371-380), in Rowley (*The Relevance of Apocalyptic,* London, 1947, pp. 84-90). See also Lods, *Histoire de la littérature hébraïque et juive,* Paris, 1950 p. 816).

The dates suggested range from the fourth century, B.C., to the last half of the first century, A.D. But the central —

and reasonable — area over which critical opinion oscillates is the first two centuries, B.C., between the time of the Machabees and the rise to power of Herod, the Idumaean, in 37, B.C. This *terminus ad quem* is based on the allusion in Jub., 35,23 and 38,14 to the submission of the sons of Edom (the Idumaeans) to the sons of Jacob "up to the present day." The majority of critics, however, does not go beyond 100 B.C., for — apart from the difficult chapter 23 — all the discoverable historical allusions refer to the second century. The *terminus a quo* is obtained by the obvious allusions to the persecutions of Antiochus Epiphanes and the Machabean wars.

One remark should be made concerning the *terminus a quo*. In chapters 37 and 38 of *Jubilees,* the war of the sons of Jacob against the sons of Esau presents surprising similarities to that of Judas Machabeus against the Edomites; and, conversely, it appears that the action of Judas Machabeus, in its literary presentations, has been influenced by the memory of Juda, the son of Jacob. In Hebrew, the two names are exactly the same.

The account in *Genesis* merely mentions the rivalry of Esau and Jacob. In *Jubilees,* the *sons of Esau,* more wicked than their father, take the initiative in attack (37,1-5); they form an alliance with the surrounding nations (the Ammonites, the Moabites, the Philistines, the Kittim...) (37,6-10). The *sons of Jacob* fight beside their father and the principal role falls to *Juda* (38,1-5) who leads the troops. This may be compared with the account in I Mac., 5,1-3:

"When the nations round about heard that the altar and the sanctuary were built up as before, they were exceedingly angry. And they thought to destroy *the generation of*

126

Jacob that were among them, and they began to kill some of the people, and to persecute them. Then Judas fought against *the children of Esau* in Idumaea, and them that were in Acrabathane; because they beset the Israelites round about."

In both episodes it is the figure of Juda(s) who is in the foreground. He leads the sons of Jacob to victory over the sons of Esau.

The same ambivalence of the figure of Juda is to be found in the *Chronicles of Jerahmeel*, a Hebrew collection of Jewish traditions, of different periods and very unequal value, parts of which, however, are remarkably close to Machabean traditions and to the *Book of Jubilees*. (cf. Gaster, *The Chronicles of Jerahmeel*, London, 1899, pp. 84-87).

Judas Machabeus was the savior of Israel (I Mac., 9,21); likewise, in *Jubilees*, Jacob prophesied to his son, Juda:

"You will be the help of Jacob, and in you Israel will find her salvation" (Jub., 31,19).

The image of the lion, characteristic of Juda in the prophecy of Jacob (Gen., 49,9), is applied to Judas Machabeus:

"In his acts he was like a lion, and like a lion's whelp roaring for his prey.... He grieved many kings, and made *Jacob* glad with his works" (I Mac., 3,4 and 7). (Cf. Gaster, *The Chronicles*...p. 271).

It is not to be doubted, consequently, that the prophecies concerning Juda, the son of Jacob, were transferred to the

127

person of Judas Machabeus; the messianic hopes were laid, at least momentarily, upon Judas Machabeus. It is noteworthy that, in the *Chronicles of Jerahmeel*, he is given the title of "the anointed of the battle" (ch. 94 and 95) (ibid., pp. 276-279).

APPENDIX II

TEXTS RELATING TO
A SOLAR CYCLE OF 28 YEARS,
BEGINNING ON WEDNESDAY,
IN JUDAISM

1. *Talmud of Babylon*

In Berakhot 59b is reported the opinion of Abay, a Babylonian amora (end of third — beginning of fourth century).

"The rabbis taught: Seeing the sun in its *tequfah* (solstice or equinox), the moon in its strength, the stars on their course, and the planets following their order, a man will say: Blessed be the Author of creation. When does this come about? Abay said: Every 28 years, when the cycle returns and when the *tequfah* of Nisan (spring equinox)

129

arrives in Saturn, in the *night of the third to the fourth day.*"

This passage is to be found among the blessings for creation, an implicit reference to the text of *Genesis*. The beginning of the cycle had to take place at the full moon ("the moon in its strength").

A commentary of Rashi on this passage traces the cycle back to the Babylonian, Samuel Yarhina'ah (end of second century).

2. *Pirqe Rabbi Eliezer*

According to Friedlander, whose translation we follow here (*Pirqe Rabbi Eliezer*, London, 1916), and according to the common opinion, the *pirqe* represent a *Palestinian* tradition. Friedlander also indicates at some length the literary affinities which exist, in spite of polemical points, between this apocryphal work and works such as *Jubilees*, *I* and *II Henoch*, the *Testaments of the XII Patriarchs*, the Syriac *Apocalypse of Barach*, the *Book of Wisdom*, the *Book of Adam and Eve* (Introd., pp. xxi-liii). All of these works are of particular interest to us, having been transmitted by a Christian group.

In a chapter on creation are to be found texts relating to the paths of the moon and of the sun. In relation to the fourth day of creation a long description is given of the solar and planetary cycles.[1] The great cycle of the sun takes 28 years, comprising 7 smaller cycles, each of 4 years. The number of days in the solar year is 364¼; each of the 4 seasons of the year has 91 days, 7½ hours. The first cycle of 4 years commences *at the beginning of the fourth day,* at the *tequfah* of Nisan. The second cycle commences with 5 days' displacement (4 X 1¼ days) at the beginning of the 2nd day of the week; the third at the beginning of the 7th day, and so on, through the 5th, 3rd, 1st and 6th days. After 7 cycles of 4 years, "at the end of the 35 (intercalated) days" of the great 28-year cycle, the cycle of the *tequfah* recommences *"at the beginning of the 4th day,* at the hour of Saturn, at the hour of its creation" (ibid., pp. 34-37. Certain passages are obscure and have evidently suffered in the transmission of the text.).

This intercalation of 35 days is noteworthy. Evidently, it bridges the gap between 28 years of 364 days and the solar cycle. Nothing is said of the way in which these 35 days were distributed; but since they form an exact number of weeks (5 weeks), the system of intercalation would correspond easily to a calendar of the type of *Jubilees.*

The paths of the moon must also have their point of departure at the beginning of the night of Wednesday; but it is difficult to be certain whether it is a question of a new moon or a full moon, as was the case with the Magarya (pp. 43-50). In order to have the length of the solar coincide with that of the lunar cycle it was necessary to employ a cycle of 84 years. Then the sun and the moon would once more coincide:

> *"at the beginning of the eve of the fourth day,* at the hour of Saturn, *at the hour of their creation"* (p. 49).

3. *Al-Biruni*

In a chapter of his *Chronology of the Eastern nations,* where he treats of the Jewish computations as a whole,

Al-Biruni mentions, after several Jewish cycles, other cycles known as *tequfoth,* "the *tequfah* signifying the beginning of each of the four parts of the year."

The Jews calculate the intervals between two *tequfoth* either scientifically, in a manner identical to that of Ptolemy — and, in this case, the intervals between two *tequfoth* are irregular — or else approximately — and, in this case, the interval between two *tequfoth* is one of 91 days, 7½ hours (*Chronology*, pp. 162-163).

A few pages later, Al-Biruni indicates how, in practice, the Jews calculate the *tequfoth* of a year:

"If the Jews wish to find the quarter-years, or *tequfoth,* of any year, they take the years of the era of Adam, including the current year, and they convert them into solar cycles (dividing them by 28). As for the years left over, the count for each year is 30 hours, that is, 1¼ days. They ignore the number of weeks contained in this total, so that finally they obtain a number of days less than seven. Then, either they count these days from the *beginning of the night of Wednesday,* or else they add 3 and count the total thus obtained from the beginning of the night of Sunday. This gives them the *tequfoth* of Nisan, that is, the spring equinox, of the year in question....

They count the total of days from the *beginning of the night* of Wednesday, because *certain* of them maintain that the sun was created on Wednesday, 27 Elul, and that the *tequfoth* of Tishri (autumn equinox) took place at the end of the third hour of Wednesday, 5 Tishri. Furthermore, they make the sun pass through the two quarter-years of spring and summer in 182 days, 15

132

hours, if they are not calculating with mathematical precision, as we have already seen. Now, if we convert these 182 days, 15 hours, into weeks, the days disappear and we are left with only 15 hours. If we then calculate backwards from the *tequfah* of Tishri, counting this number of hours, we come to the beginning of the first hour of the night of Wednesday. And it is from this moment that the calculation spoken of begins.

Other Jews hold that the sun was created in the first part of the Ram, at the moment from which the calculation of the *tequfoth* starts, and that it was in conjunction with the moon ... (ibid., p. 168).

In this text, which is not uniformly clear, are once again to be found the notions already encountered in *Pirqe Rabbi Eliezer*. The calculation is still based on the difference between a year of 364 days and a year of 365¼ days, that is 1¼ days, or 30 hours. At the end of 28 years of 364 days, the difference with the solar cycle forms an exact number of weeks The elimination, in the calculation of the *tequfoth*, of the exact number of weeks formed by the sum of the annual 30 supplementary hours, manifests very clearly the concern that the calculations should be brought back to a point of departure which is always the same day of the week; and this point of departure is still the beginning of the night of *Wednesday*. Sunday, the first day of creation, is secondary in relation to Wednesday since it is obtained only by a supplementary addition. It is, nevertheless, taking Sunday as the point of departure that Al-Biruni draws up the table of *tequfoth* which follows this passage. This proves that the Jews commonly calculated from Sunday. This makes it all the more significant when Al-Biruni feels compelled to point out the greater antiquity of the calculation from Wednesday.

To which Wednesday do these calculations refer? Without any doubt, it is to that which immediately precedes the spring equinox (para. 1).[2] Yet the second paragraph rather curiously superimposes heterogeneous concepts, one on the other. The creation of the sun on Wednesday is dated 27 Elul; the autumn equinox is placed 8 days later, a Wednesday, 5 Tishri, (Elul having 29 days) at the end of the third hour of the day, that is to say, 15 hours after the beginning of the night of Wednesday, 5. Now we ask: why should there be this backward calculation of two quarter-years (spring and summer), if it is not to get back to the point of departure of the calculation, to the spring equinox? This point of departure, 182 days earlier, appears to be inspired by a calendar of the type of *Jubilees* with its trimestral time-units of 91 days (quarter-year) which begin on Wednesday, 1/I. In fact, however, in a Jewish calendar of lunar months, by counting back from the beginning of the night of 5 Tishri to 1 Nisan, inclusive, one would obtain a total of only 181 days.[3] In a calendar of the type of *Jubilees* the interval between the two halves of the year is one of 182 days. Here there seem to be two types of calendar, superimposed one on the other, one of them based on the lunar month, beginning in autumn, the other based on the sun — with four seasons — which begins in spring and of which only residual elements remain.

In the third paragraph, the author mentions that certain Jews held that the sun had been created in the first part of the Ram, thus at the beginning of spring. Jewish tradition hesitated between these two dates for the birth of the world.[4]

It appears, accordingly, that two important consequences may be drawn. The first is that we have indirect evidence, as in *Pirqe Rabbi Eliezer*, of the survival of elements of a computation related to that of *Jubilees*. This computation was based essentially on the week, and its primary concern was to refer calculations to a *fixed* day of the week. The second consequence is that, in an ancient Jewish ambient — prior to the usage to which Al-Biruni refers — the point of departure of the computation commonly adopted was a Wednesday, at the beginning of spring. Thus we have proof, drawn from the whole of the texts assembled, of the existence of a broad, common Jewish base for a calendar beginning on Wednesday.

It would be most interesting to know the origin of the 28-year cycle found here. A similar 28-year cycle is encountered in Church writers. Normally it is explained by the comment, attributed to the Christian calculators who authored the perpetual calendars, that at the end of 28 Julian years of 365¼ days, the days of the week recommenced in the same order at the beginning of the 29th year. Yet no information is to be found on the origin of the Christian cycle of 28 years. An attempt should be made to show whether any link is to be found between the Christian cycle and the Jewish cycle of the same length.

The 28-year calculation, based solely on the week, cannot be properly explained apart from reference to circles where the day of the week which began the year took on a very special significance. Although Rashi knows only a Babylonian author of the second century, one would be inclined to suspect an earlier origin in a Jewish environment. The Jewish calculators, wishing to restore harmony between the 364-day calendar and the solar year, were aware — with or without the aid of the Julian calendar — that it was necessary to intercalate 5 weeks in 28 years. The difficulty is that, up to the present, there is nowhere any evidence in pre-Christian Judaism of a cycle of 28 years, nor of an intercalation of 5 weeks or 35 days. As regards the cycle of 84 years, on the contrary, considered in the *Pirqe Rabbi Eliezer* as a multiple of the 28-year cycle, certain Christian authors speak of Jewish influences.[5]

APPENDIX III

THE LUNAR QUESTION

THE lunar question is posed most forcefully with regard to the note, already quoted, of Al-Biruni on the Magarya. For the Magarya:

> "Festivals are legal only when the moon appears full in Palestine during the night of the Wednesday which follows the day of Tuesday, after the setting of the sun. This is their New Year's Day. It is from this day that the days and the months are counted and that the annual cycle of feasts begins. For God created the two great lights of heaven on a Wednesday."

The Karaite writer, Qirqisani, adds on the subject of the Magarya:

> "The moon is never larger than when it is full. That took place on the fourth day of creation, yet this does not prevent it being the first day of the month" (cf. *R. B.*, LVII (1950), p. 422).[1]

These texts raise several questions.

a) A full moon on the fourth day of creation?

This belief is *not peculiar to the Magarya*. Probably it is the primitive idea of those Jewish groups who made the fourth day the point of departure for the solar computation. Abay states clearly: "the moon in its strength" (see Appendix II). In the *Pirqe* and the text of Al-Biruni, the sun starts out in conjunction with the moon; but there is no way of telling whether this is a full moon. However, analogy and "logic" would seem to prove that it is. For from the very beginning the moon ought to have performed her functions worthily! God could create the stars only in their full perfection, as Qirqisani states explicitly.

Now, the idea that the moon was full on the fourth day of creation is found once again in *ancient Christian authors,* except that, with them, the anniversary of this fourth day of creation is Easter. Thus the *De Pascha computus*:

> "The moon, created five days before the Kalends of April" (*C.S.E.L.* 3,3, p. 253).

Since the world was created at the spring equinox — hence eight days before the Kalends of April (25 March), according

138

to the official date of the Julian calendar — a Sunday, naturally — five days before the Kalends of April represents a Wednesday. Similarly, Quintus Julius Hilarianus:

"On the fourth day, that is, five days before the Kalends of April, the moon was created towards the evening, the 14th, so as to give light to the darkness of that first night. ...God willed that the week of the Pasch should begin at the fourteenth moon towards the evening so that, when the day of the Pasch dawned, which is the first of the same week, the fifteenth moon might be for them the first day of unleavened bread" (*Expositum de die Paschae. P.L.* 13, 1109).

It is quite a striking fact that from these two texts it emerges indirectly — this time for lunar reasons — that the ideal day for the Jewish Pasch was a Wednesday, the anniversary of the full moon of the creation.[2] One might also add the fascinating story of a synod, said to have been held at Caesarea by Theophilus, at which the bishops discussed the date of Easter: The moon was created full, as was fitting (*P.G.* 5, 1368).

The association made by Christian writers between the moon of the fourth day of creation and the paschal moon leads to a new question:

b) A full moon at the beginning or in the middle of the month?

In the case of Christians, since for them it is question of the paschal moon, it is evidently the moon of the middle of the month (14 or 15 of the month). But the texts on the Magarya state that there it is a question of the full moon at the beginning of the month and of the year. This might appear extremely curious; yet certain scholars have expressed the view that such a system existed in Judaism (cf. Encyclopedia judaica, art. Kalender, IX, 798)[3] and we find evidence of it in ancient authors.

On the Christian side, we may notice once again Q. Julius Hilarianus:

"Whilst there was still no law given by the Lord Almighty, men often hesitated about the course of the moon. Some called it the first day of the month when the full moon appeared, such as it had appeared for the world upon the command of God; others held another opinion" (ibid., c. 1107).

On the Jewish side, an astonishing text has been cited by Poznanski. It concerns Yefet and Yeshoua ben Yahouda who speak of those Jews who are partisans of the full moon at the beginning of the month. Yefet, in his commentary on Gen., 1,14, declares that there are no longer any such people. But the glossator of Yefet's words realizes that it was the "Sadducees" who were referred to:

"The words of the wise man (Yefet) refer to those who consider as the first night of the new month that in which the moon becomes full, that is, the 15th night. These words refute those who make themselves guilty of lying and of false testimony by claiming that the Karaites are the same as the Sadducees. For, if this were true, we ought to imitate the latter when they begin the (religious) month in the middle of the (astronomical) month. In fact, we act in quite another fashion." (*R.E.J.* XLIV (1902), pp. 171-172.

Who are these remarkable "Sadducees" with whom the Karaites refuse to be identified? It is impossible not to think of the Magarya-Qumranians.[4] But this raises another question:

c) *How can a conjunction with the moon occur in a solar calendar?*

Since a year of twelve lunar months gives a total of 354 days, it is evidently impossible, if a conjunction occurs in the first year, that it should again occur in at least the two following years, with a solar calendar of 364 days. It must, then, be supposed that the Magarya were concerned with rediscovering the *ideal* conjunction of the fourth day of creation. But it may still be asked how they achieved it in practice.[5] Possibly ch. 74 of the *Luminaries of Henoch* represents an attempt to meet this desire; but the present state of the text is too confused for it to be of much help by itself. In any event, it proves that the courses of the moon held considerable importance for the followers of its calendar. During at least one whole period of the history of the sect, consequently, special importance was attached to conjunctions with the moon. This should be kept in mind, primarily because of the anti-lunar polemic of *Jubilees*.

The lunar problem must now be placed in another fashion, with the aid of *Jubilees* and of the biblical texts themselves.

141

In the *priestly account of creation* the moon is placed on the same footing as the other heavenly lights to serve as a sign "for the times (mw'dy), for the days, for the years" (Gen., 1,14). There is no mention of the months. The role of the moon could be limited to distinguishing day from night or giving light to the night (Gen., 1,16); but it is not excluded that it might play a role in the *mw'dym,* the precise meaning of which has to be determined, but which must have a liturgical character in the present texts (in Ps., 104,19, the *mw'dym* are related to the moon.). The LXX translate as *kairous* (interpreted as "seasons" in Philo, *De Opificio,* 59. See also Gal., 4,10). If we admit that the moon plays role in the *mw'dy* of Gen., 1,14, it may not, perhaps, be necessary to have recourse to the composite character of the priestly documents to explain this fact.

Jubilees intentionally modifies the account of Gen., 1,14-18. The sun alone has the function

> "of being a great light over the earth for the days, the sabbaths, the months, the festivals, the years, the sabbaths of years, the jubilees and for all the seasons of the year" (Jub., 2,9).

Stern reproaches are addressed to:

> "those who base their observations on the moon — which disturbs the seasons and arrives from year to year ten days too soon" (Jub., 6,36).

These texts are evidently to be explained in terms of a violent polemic against the use of lunar months in the religious calendar. Since it is also said that

142

"all the children of Israel shall forget the way of the years" (Jub., 6,34. Cf. *CDC* III,14: *"all* Israel has gone astray"),

it seems very likely that *Jubilees* represents an extremist re-action advocating a return to strict orthodoxy in the face of a fairly general lunar practice. The polemical character of these texts is too pronounced for one to draw the conclusion from them that the calendar which they defend was never con-cerned with the conjunction of the moon.[6]

It would evidently be necessary to determine exactly the meaning of *hodesh* (new moon or month) in several passages of the Bible. The "new moons" play a large role, even for the priestly writers. For example in Ezech., 45,17; 46,1-6; I Par., 2,3; 8,13; 23,31; 31,3; I Esd., 3,5; Neh., 10,34. What is the meaning of the word *hodesh* in these passages? Comparison must be made with the characteristic formula of *Numbers* "the heads of your months" (Num., 10,10; 28,11) or with the expression, "the first of the month," found very frequently in the priestly form of numbering. We have already seen the capital importance of these first days of the month — and especially of the trimester — in the calendar of *Jubilees*. Are we to think that in the priestly calendar *hodesh* has simply the sense of "first day"? Or is it that the custom was always maintained, even during the dominant period of the calendar, of celebrating "new moons" which did not coincide with the first days of the month of the 364-day calendar? The latter hypothesis seems likely. The festivals of the new moon were certainly deeply rooted in the Semitic way of life. After the Exile, the lunar calendar must have been used as the civil calendar, the priestly calendar being employed only for liturgical ceremonies. A better understanding is thus obtained of the internal evolution which must have taken place in the liturgy of the Temple towards the fourth or third centuries. It was an easier thing to resume use of a lunar calendar which had never completely ceased to exist.

The mention of twenty-six classes of priests in 1 *QM* II 2, as opposed to the twenty-four classes of I Par., 24,7-8, was at first interpreted as a clash between the solar and the lunar calendar. For the twenty-six classes of priests can be justified only in the context of a solar calendar (exactly 52 weeks for 364 days; 2 weeks for each class). But the discovery in 4Q of a recent document, reported by Mr. Milik in a communication, shows that a system of twenty-four classes is compatible with a solar calendar of 364 days within a six-year cycle. Consequently, one may not, as I previously thought, use this fact to argue that an internal evolution from a solar to a lunar system is to be discovered in the books of *Paralipomenon*. The work of the Chronicler may, then, use the Babylonian names of the months (cf. Esd., 6,15; Neh., 1,1; 2,1; 6,15), but there is no justification in this for finding elements in liturgical usage contrary to the old priestly calendar.

At the beginning of the second century, Sirach, whose priestly affinities are known, bears witness to the role of the moon in Jewish festivities. In Ecclus., 43,6-8 (Greek), the moon gives the signal for festivals and marks out the times; the corresponding Hebrew passage is rather confused, but it seems to assign to the moon the function of determining the months. In Ecclus., 50,6, the Hebrew makes clear that the moon is full "on festival days." Given the doubtful nature of the Hebrew text of *Ecclesiasticus,* it would be very useful to know which edition a group like that of Qumran could have possessed.[7]

But no passage of *Ecclesiasticus* is opposed to the hypothesis of a modified calendar.

We shall, doubtless, always remain in ignorance about the degree to which the old priestly calendar had evolved at the beginning of the second century. A likely solution would be that the celebration of feasts on fixed days was preserved for a very long time. For the three liturgical days were much more closely attached to the sabbatical week than to the 364-day calendar. Perhaps they were equally tied to the 50-day unit of time. But *the stability of these liturgical days made them capable of detaching themselves from such temporary supports and frameworks.* In any event, they were destined to survive in the Christian liturgy in a 364-day calendar. It is, accordingly, quite possible that, while maintaining the festivals on fixed days of the week, the attempt was made to link them with the full moon. It was simple to choose for the Pasch or the Feast of Tabernacles the Wednesday which immediately preceded the full moon so that this moon fell within the seven days of the feast. This presupposes the dropping of the numeral system and the adoption of Babylonian names for the months, even for religious purposes. The "lunar" passages of *Ecclesiasticus* can be well explained in terms of an intermediary form of calendar such as this.

It may, then, be admitted that when a profound difference arose over the days of the week, certain groups preserved this form of modified calendar, and followed the practice of reckoning from Wednesday. There must have been several variants of the fixed-day type calendar in existence. So far Qumran appears to have been very conservative; but the notices on the Magarya and the "Sadducees" left by the glossator on Yefet do not rule out the possibility that they may

145

have adopted certain lunar modifications and were not simply concerned with a conjunction of the moon.

Coming to the Christian calendar, the texts quoted above on the paschal moon appear to supply adequate proof that the feast of Easter has always been associated with a full moon. Whether in an earlier form of Judaism this paschal moon was that of the beginning or that of the middle of the month remains in question. Other reasons lead one to believe that the Christian calendar grew out of a form of Jewish calendar which had already undergone modification (cf. p. 64).

NOTES

INTRODUCTION

1. A. Jaubert, "Le calendrier des Jubilés et de la secte de Qumrân. Ses origines bibliques," *V.T.* III (1953), pp. 250-264. "La date de la dernière Cène," *R.H.R.* CXLVI (1954), pp. 140-173. "Le calendrier des Jubilés et les jours liturgiques de la semaine," *V.T.* VII (1957), pp. 35-61. Certain pages of these articles have been reproduced verbatim with the kind permission of Presses Universitaires, Paris (*R.H.R.*) and Brill, Leyde (*V.T.*)

FIRST PART

CHAPTER ONE

1. We possess *Jubilees* only in two translations. Fragments found at Qumran confirm the already well-founded opinion that the original was Hebrew. There remain extant an Ethiopian and a Latin translation, the latter fragmentary; both are based on a Greek translation of the Hebrew. Ethiopic text: Charles, *The ethiopic version of the Hebrew Book of Jubilees,* Oxford, 1895; English translation: Charles, *The Book of Jubilees,* London, 1902, and *Apocrypha and Pseudopigrapha of the O. T.,* t. II, Oxford, 1913; German: Littmann in Kautzsch, *Die Apocryphen und Pseudepigraphen des A. T.,* Tubingen, 1900 and 1921, t. II. Latin text: Charles, ibid.; Roensch, *Das Buch der Jubilaen,* Leipzig, 1874. See information on Greek and Syriac fragments, and bibliography, in *D.B.S.,* t. I, 377-380.

2. Cf. *R.B.,* LXIII (1956), pp. 54, 60.

3. So, Fr. Milik in his communication to the *O.T.* congress (Strasbourg), August 28, 1956. See *Supplements to V.T.,* IV, Leyde, 1957, pp. 24-26.

4. On the sacred character of the calendar, cf. A. Dupont - Sommer, "Contribution a l'exégèse du Manuel de Discipline X 1-8," *V.T.*, II (1952), pp. 229-230, and *Nouveaux aperçus sur les manuscrits de la mer Morte*, Paris, 1953, pp. 145-146.

5. I Hen., 43,2. Cf. Jub., 2,2, where the angels are placed before the "spirits of all creatures, including "cold, heat, spring, summer, fall and winter." The close ties between stars and angels in antiquity require no comment; cf. Job 38,7: "When the morning stars praised me together, and all the sons of God made a joyful melody."

6. I Hen., 81,2; Jub., 6,17.23.35.

7. Jub., 10,10-14; 12,27; 21,10; 25,7; 39,6; cf. 32,21-26.

8. I Hen., 72,13-32; 82,10-18. The intercalary day is the last of the month; this is perfectly clear in the texts of *I Henoch* and may easily be deduced from Jub., 6,23-32; see on this point my reply to Mr. Morgenstern in *V.T.* VII (1957), pp. 35-44.

9. Since the year must always begin on the same day of the week, one may suggest the intercalation either of blank days or else of entire *weeks*, possibly after sabbaths of years, considered as units of time. These intercalations would be possible between the four seasons of the year; see above, page 47. See also the intercalations of 5 weeks every 28 years in the solar 28-year cycle (App. II). The method of intercalation may have varied at different times.

10. Ex., 23,16; 34,22; Num., 28,26 (Cf. Deut., 16,9; Lev., 23,10-21).

11. Jub., 44,1-8. This is the only text which enables us to fix by deduction the date of the Feast of Weeks exactly on the 15th of the month! "Israel departed . . . on the first day of month III; . . . at the Well of the Oath he offered a sacrifice on the 7th of the month. . . . He remained there 7 days . . . *and he celebrated the feast of the harvest* of the first fruits. . . . And on the 16th day the Lord appeared to him. . . . And Israel left the Well of the Oath on the 16th day of the month."

12. Cf. Nemoy, *Karaite Anthology* New Haven, 1952, pp. 50, 216, 222.

13. Cf. Pedersen, *Israel. Its life and its culture*, t. II, London - Copenhagen, 1940, p. 303 and p. 696, n. 1.

14. Epstein went only half way; he had discovered that in *Jubilees* Pentecost must always fall on a Sunday, interpreting Jub., 6,20 of the *first* day of the week (*R.E.J.*,–XXII [1891], pp. 4-8).

15. Barthélémy, "Notes en marge de publications récentes sur les manuscrits de Qumrân," *R.B.* LIX (1952), pp. 199-203.

Notes

16. The same as the Magarya. Cf. De Vaux, "A propos des manuscrits de la mer Morte," *R.B.* LVII (1950), p. 423.

17. Al-Biruni is treated at length in the translation of E. Sachau, *The Chronology of Ancient Nations,* London, 1879, p. 278. This text has already been noticed by Poznanski, "Philon dans l'ancienne littérature judeo-arabe," *R.E.J.,* L (1905), p. 17.

18. In her book, *La notion d'Alliance dans le judaïsme aux abords de l'ere chrétienne,* Paris, Le Seuil, 1963, p. 90, no. 5, the author, following Jewish parallels and other works, interprets somewhat differently the chronology of Abraham's journey. The days begin with the evening watch. The intervention of Mastéma must be placed on the night preceding the 12th of the month. Abraham departs the morning of the 12th and arrives at Mount Sion on the third day, that is, the 14th. The sacrifice of Isaac (the evening of the 14th) corresponds to the sacrifice of the Pasch. The next day, the 15th, Abraham sets out again and ought to be back on the third day, which would be the 17th. Abraham's journey covers therefore the entire week from the 12th to the 17th of the first month and would fall exactly between two sabbaths, as the following table shows.

19. It is to be observed that these results cannot be due to chance. Apart from the certain halt on 14/III, the journey of Abraham and Isaac (Jub., 18,1-17, cf. 17,15) is situated between two sabbaths; and this appears to be true also of the journey of Jacob (Jub., 44,1). The author is consciously obeying a certain plan.

20. This is the method which Mr. Morgenstern employed in "The calendar of the Book of Jubilees, its origin and its character," *V.T.* V (1955), pp. 34-76; but his table is inaccurate because of an error in placing the intercalary day.

21. This is the biblical date, cf. Ex., 12,6; Lev., 23,5; Num., 9,3.5.11; Jos., 5,10, etc. ... but as days began the previous evening (cf. Lev., 23,32), the *feast* of the Pasch occurs on the 15th (Wednesday). It is not agreed at what precise moment of the evening the day of the 15th began.

22. See tables at end of book.

23. Dates of birth of the patriarchs: Ruben 14/IX (Saturday), Simeon 21/X (Tuesday), Levi 1/I (Wednesday), Juda 15/III (Sunday), Dan 9/VI (Monday), Nephthali 5/VII (Sunday), Gad 12/VIII (Tuesday), Aser 2/XI Saturday), Issachar 4/V (Monday), Zabulon 7/VII (Tuesday), Joseph 1/IV (Wednesday) — according to Jub., 28,11-24. Benjamin 11/VIII (Monday) — according to Jub., 32,33. Unless there is an error in transmission of the manuscripts, Ruben and Aser

were born on the sabbath day, which appears strangely unfitting. A birth on the sabbath meant a violation of the day. The most fitting day of birth was undoubtedly *Wednesday* (cf. Str-Bill. II 405). "It was the practice of the ancient *hasidim* to exercise their conjugal rights only on Wednesday, so as to avoid defilement for their wives on the sabbath" (*Nidda* 38ab), a view based on the calculation of the number of days between conception and birth according to the preceding explanation of *Nidda*. Cf., in Jub., 50,8 the prohibition of conjugal relations on the sabbath day.

CHAPTER TWO

1. Cf. Barthélémy, ibid., *R.B.*, LIX (1952), pp. 201-202, who protests against the hypothesis of a utopian calendar.

2. Sons of Levi (Jub., 45,16; *IQSa* I 220. Sons of Sadoc (*IQS* V 2. 9; *CDC* IV 3) *IQSa* I 24. II 3, etc.). Sons of Aaron (*IQS* V 21; IX 7; *IQSa* I 23, etc...).

3. On the whole, these dates have few variants. Whilst in T.M. the Flood begins the day after a sabbath, the LXX have it beginning on 27/II (Wednesday); the 27/VII of the LXX for the ark's coming to rest is probably reached by analogy. In Gen., 8,5 LXX have 1/XI (Friday). For the death of Aaron the Syriac suggests 1/I (Wednesday (cf. note 40, p. 156 for the priestly signification and the solar symbolism of this day). It is quite remarkable that even the variants appear to be confined to Wednesday and Friday.

4. It is curious to observe that according to the LXX variant in Gen., 8,5 (1/XI, Friday), the distance from the following date, 1/I, is one of 61 days in the *Jubilee* calendar (30 plus 31). Now this interval of 61 days coincides exactly with the time given in Gen., 8,6-12 (document J), if it be recalled that to 40 days are to be added 3 periods of 7 days (21 days). The variant evidenced by the Greek might well be of ancient origin and correspond to a desire to unify the documents.

The hypothesis advanced above does not resolve all the problems posed by the chronology of the Flood. The departure on 17/II remains mysterious; the author could have chosen another Sunday (the same date appears in Jub., 3,17, for Eve's temptation!). Furthermore, it has been very pertinently maintained—in the hypothesis of lunar months—that from 17/II, when the Flood began, to 27/II, when it ended, there

Notes

was a period of 12 lunar months (354 days), plus 10 days, that is, in all, 364 days. This would indicate that the author was making use of lunar months, but at the same time wished to assign to the Flood the duration of a solar year of 364 days. Lunar months are certainly eliminated by the 150 days; yet it is not impossible that we have here a deliberate combination of two calendars.

Moreover there exist certain differences between the priestly chronology of the Flood and that of *Jubilees*. *Jubilees* add several dates to the Masoretic Text. a) To the two first days of seasons mentioned in the Masoretic Text. 1/X and 1/I (Gen., 8,5.13), *Jubilees add* 1/IV and 1/VII (Jub., 5,29; cf. 6,26), with the very clear intention that these four first days of the trimesters be celebrated as days of remembrance (Jub., 6,25.28). b) In the Masoretic Text the earth is dry on 27/II (Wednesday); in *Jubilees* the date is 17/II (Sunday), 27/II being celebrated as the day of leaving the ark (Jub., 5, 31-32). c) In *Jubilees* Noah enters the ark from 1/II (Sunday) to 16 (Saturday) (Jub., 5,23); this is probably to be taken as up to 16, exclusive, since this is a sabbath. In the *Book of Adam and Eve* (cf. above, pp. 55-56) the ark is entered on a Friday.

Finally there is a textual difficulty concerning the date of closing the ark in Jub., 5,23, that is to say, concerning the beginning of the Flood. The figure 17 is given in the Ethiopic edition of Charles (this has been kindly verified by Mr. Velat) as in the Masoretic Text. The figure 27 (LXX) is given in the translation of Kautzch and by several commentators (cf. *International Critical Commentary. Genesis,* Edinburgh, 1930, p. 167, note). Given the preceding reference to 16, it is, doubtless, the Masoretic date, 17, which is to be chosen.

5. Several interesting liturgical points may be noticed. In II Par., 7,10, the people are dismissed on 23/VII (Thursday), the day following a great fifteen days of festivity, running from 8/VII to 22/VII (Wednesday to Wednesday). In Par., 29,17: beginning of purifications on 1/I (Wednesday); entry into the portico on 8/I (Wednesday); purifications completed 16/I (Thursday), the day after the Pasch. In II Chron., 30, 15. 21. 23, after the second Pasch, sacrificed on Thursday evening (14/II), two weeks of festivity begin on Friday.

6. Cf. Baillet, "Fragments araméens de Qumrân 2," *R.B.* LXII (1955), pp. 222-245.

7. Wednesday, Friday or Sunday.

8. Might this be an exception in the Masoretic Text to the rule of arrivals on Friday? However, the stress is on the oracle, not on the arrival.

151

The Date of the Last Supper

9. It is probably necessary to fix *Rosh hashana* (the first of the year) in the VII month of the year, in accordance with the current interpretation of the expression in later Judaism. It should, however, be observed, that in Hen., 82,15, the "head" of the year is placed in spring. But, whatever be its meaning in Ezechiel, since the two semesters are perfectly symmetrical in a calendar of Jubilees-type, the distribution of days to months is always the same, and 10/I would also fall on Friday.

10. It might be asked whether, in this system, Tuesday had not a particular importance. The Pasch was sacrificed on Tuesday evening; the seventh day of the Pasch was a Tuesday; so also was the seventh day of the Feast of Tabernacles, before the introduction of the octave. Three out of four of the visions of Aggeus will be placed on Tuesday—one of them on the seventh day of Tabernacles (cf. below, note 29, p. 155). The only date given in *I Henoch* is that of a vision, 14/VII (Tuesday), eve of the Feast of Tabernacles (cf. below, note 42, p. 157).

11. Ex., 1,8; 37, 9; 42,16-20; 47; 48. Compare, in Num., 2, the disposition of the tribes around the Tent, according to the four points of the compass.

12. Mr. Morgenstern thinks that the calendar of the first Temple was a solar one, borrowed from the Phoenicians by Solomon. It was thus based on observation of the solstices and equinoxes. The Temple would have been built in such a way that, on the two days of the equinox, the sun shone directly through the eastern gate (this, following late witnesses, mostly rabbinical). See Morgenstern, "The gates of righteousness," *H.U.C.A.* VI (1929), pp. 1-37, and *V.T.* V (1955), pp. 68-69.

14. "It has been pointed out that there are four constellations, at more or less 90 degrees from each other at the equator (which the ancient Babylonians considered rather than the ecliptic), all of them containing one star which attracts attention; these are the Lion and the Scorpion, these being diametrically opposed, the Bull and Pegasus. Their names are very ancient. Originally, the Scorpion was a Man-Scorpion, and Pegasus, the winged horse, could suggest an Eagle, particularly since there is another constellation already bearing this name in Babylon." Allo, *Saint Jean. L'Apocalypse,* Paris, 1933, p. 72, on Apoc., 4,7. Cf. Lohmeyer, *Die Offenbarung des Johannes,* Tübingen, 1953, p. 48. On the signs of the zodiac among the ancient Jews, cf. Driver, "Two astronomical passages in the Old Testament," *J.T.S.* VII, 1 (New series, April, 1956), pp. 1-11.

15. Gen., 7,11, departure of the ark, 17/II (Sunday). Esd., 8,31, departure from Ahava, 12/I (Sunday). Jub., 44,1, departure of Jacob,

Notes

1/III (Sunday). Gen., 8,4, halt of the ark on Mt. Ararat, 17/VII (Friday). Ex., 16,1, arrival in the desert of Sin, 15/II (Friday). Jos., 4,19, arrival in the Promised Land, 10/I (Friday). Esd., 7,9, arrival of Esdras in Jerusalem, 1/V (Friday), etc.

16. This mysticism of the number four will reappear in the *tetractys* of the Pythagorians. As far as the fourth day is concerned, there is to be found only the distant parallel of the fourth day of the month. In Babylon, the great poem of creation, *Enuma Elish,* was read in its entirety on the fourth day of the feast of the New Year (4 Nisan). For Egypt, cf. Plutarch: "It is said that Horus, the son of Isis, was the first who sacrificed to the sun on the fourth day" (*Isis and Osiris,* 52). Compare also the importance of the fourth day in the curious catalog of days attributed to Hesido (*The works and the days,* 770, 798, 800, 809, 819).

17. The beginning of the night of Wednesday (Tuesday evening) is the moment of the week furthest removed from both the preceding and the following Saturday; it is, consequently, the moment offering the least risk of profaning the sabbath. As the central point of a return journey undertaken between two sabbaths, it permits gatherings at a distance of three days from home; for example, for the celebration of the Pasch on Tuesday evening. (Compare Ex., 3,18 and 5,3, and, less exactly, Jub., 18,1-17.).

18. Cf. Labat, *Hémérologies et ménologies d'Assur,* Paris, 1939. The unpropitious days, which originally numbered nine, were later reduced to the following days of the month: 7th, 14th, 19th, 21st, 28th (all divisible by seven, since the 19th day is the 49th—7 X 7— of the preceding month). At a fairly early date the Chaldeans connected the days of the week with the planets (Bidez - Cumont, *Les mages hellénisés,* Paris, 1938, II, p. 229, n. 1). Later, among the Elceseans, no enterprise ought to be undertaken on the third day of the week (Hippolytus, *Elenchos,* IX,16).

19. Lewy, "The origin of the week and the oldest West Asiatic calendar," *H.U.C.A.* XVII (1942-1943), pp. 1-152. Cf. Morgenstern, *V.T.* V (1955), pp. 37 f. On the symbolism of the number *fifty* in the Mesopotamian civilizations (the God, Elil, was named "the divine Fifty"), see Lewy, p. 45; Dhorme, *Les religions de Babylonie et d'Assyrie,* coll. Mana, Paris, 1949, pp. 28, 49, 102. Regarding the number 50, Mr. Dupont - Sommer has suggested a connection with the Pythagorian doctrine ("Contribution a l'exégèse du manuel de discipline X, 1-8," *V.T.* II (1952), pp. 239-240, and *Nouveaux Aperçus,* 1953, pp. 152-156). Such resemblances are, doubtless, to be explained by the deep

153

roots which Pythagorism possessed in the ancient East (cf. above, note 16, p. 153).

20. Cf. the examples of Babylonian contracts cited by Lewy (*ibid.*, pp. 47-49) in which the calculations are based on fifty-day periods. Cf. also *The Days and the Works*, 663. For later examples among Jews and Christians, see Lewy, *ibid.*, pp. 78, 98, 103, and Morgenstern, *V.T.*, V (1955), pp. 45-54. To the texts on the Therapeuts should be added that of Saadia on Judas the Alexandrian, cited by Poznanski, *ibid.*, *R.E.J.*, L (1905), pp. 26-27: "Judas the Alexandrian said that, just as there are fifty days between the harvest of the barley and that of the wheat (from the Pasch to Pentecost), so there are fifty days between the wheat harvest and that of the must, which would fall at the end of Tamuz; likewise, the must harvest is at a distance of fifty days from that of the oil, so that the offering of oil ought to be made on 20 Elul." Compare the *Feast of Oil* in the 4Q calendar, which must fall on a *Sunday* (22/VI).

21. *Jewish Encyclopedia*, Sun (Blessing of), t. XI, 590-1591. Mr. Neher kindly permits me to add that he himself celebrated with his Jewish students the traditional blessing of the sun on *Wednesday*, April 9, 1953 (28th year of the solar cycle).

22. *Le Livre des Secrets d'Hénoch* (Vaillant edition), Paris, 1952, pp. 13,17. We consider the Slavic Henoch as a Jewish, not a Christian, writing.

23. Course of the sun: Vaillant edition, p. 13. Course of the moon, *ibid.*, pp. 15,17. The "lunar" course comprises 7 months of 31 days, 3 months of 30 days, one of 35, and one of 22: total, 364 days. See Charles, *The Book of the Secrets of Henoch*, Oxford, 1896, p. 18, note on 16,2-3. The text of the passage is, however, defective.

24. Poznanski, *ibid.*, *R.E.J.* L (1905), pp. 18-19.

25. *Ibid.*, pp. 17-18. Poznanski subsequently refers to several witnesses to an ancient solar computation (p. 19).

26. The 364 days which Lidzbarski believed he had found in certain manuscripts of the *History of Ahikar* would appear to be due to an erroneous reading. The manuscripts have the figure of 8763 hours for the year, and not 8736 (which would give 364 days); in order to obtain the latter figure a correction would have to be made. Cf. Nau, *Histoire et Sagesse d'Ahikar*, Paris, 1909, p. 229.

27. Some idea of the complexity of the problems may be obtained from a reading of the contradictory theses expressed in the various dictionaries and encyclopedias. See also Morgenstern, "The three calendars

Notes

of ancient Israel," *H.U.C.A.* I (1924), pp. 13-78; and "Supplementary Studies in the Calendar of ancient Israel," *H.U.C.A.* X (1935), pp. 1-148.

28. Capture of Jerusalem: the ninth day—no month is given in II Kings 25,3—of month IV (var. V) in Jer., 39,2 and 52, 6. The town is said to have fallen on a Thursday (var. Saturday). Burning of the Temple and the city: 10/V (Sunday) in Jer., 52,12; 7/V (Thursday) or 9/V (Saturday) in II Kings 25,8.

29. Ag., 1,1: 1/VI (Sunday); Ag., 1,15: 24/VI (Tuesday); Ag., 2,1: 21/VII (Tuesday); Ag., 2,10: 24/IX (Tuesday). Cf. note 10, p. 152

30. The converse attempt might be made to translate the Babylonian-style dates of *Esdras, Nehemias* and *Esther* into the corresponding numeral system, but the result is of little help. One date of *Esther* would certainly be opposed to the priestly calendar (Esth., 9,15).

31. We have no hesitation in citing *Judith,* the original of which is certainly Semitic.

32. This difficulty is not perhaps as insurmountable as I once believed (*V.T.* III (1953), p. 263, n. 2). The entry of Simon to the accompaniment of music and liturgical singing has every mark of a religious festival, and this would not be a work forbidden on the sabbath.

33. The only other exact date is 15 Kislev (15/IX, Sunday). The concordance of the converted dates is striking, particularly when they are compared to the dates of *Megillath Taanith* for the same period.

34. Cf. Al-Biruni, *Chronology* . . . Sachau edition, p. 86.

35. The observation of the heavenly "signs" was of great importance for *Jubilees*: "Henoch was the first to write in a book the heavenly signs according to the order of their months, so that men might know the seasons of the years according ot the order of their various months" (Jub., 4,17. Cf. Jub., 12,16 and I Henoch, 72, 14.20).

36. Cf. *Chronology* . . . pp. 277-278. The present Jewish calendar prohibits 1 Tishri falling on a Sunday, a Wednesday or a Friday, so as to avoid the Day of Expiation falling on a Sunday or a Friday and the 7th day of Tabernacles falling on a Saturday (*Jewish Encyclopedia*, Calendar, III 503). As for the day of the Pasch, the witness of Makrizi confirms that of Al-Biruni: "1 Nisan is never a Monday, a Wednesday or a Friday"; hence the same is true for 15 Nisan (de Sacy, *Chrestomathie arabe, Paris*, 1826, t. I, p. 292). The Karaite, Samuel al-Magribi, protests against the faulty rule, established by the official calendar, that the Pasch must never fall on a Monday, a Wednesday or a Friday (Nemoy, *Karaite Anthology,* p. 222). With lunar months of

155

The Date of the Last Supper

29 and 30 days alternately, if 15 Nisan fell on a Monday, then 1 Tishri would be a Wednesday and Kippur would fall on a Friday; if 15 Nisan fell on Wednesday, then 1 Tishri would be Friday and Kippur Sunday.

37. Derenbourg, *Essai sur l'histoire et la géographie de la Palestine*, t. I, Paris, 1867, p. 444, n. 6. The hesitancy about the point of departure for the 50 days of Pentecost is certainly most instructive. Whereas the calendar of *Jubilees* reckons from Sunday, 26/I, the Samaritans and the Karaites reckon from the Sunday which follows 15 Nisan (cf. de Sacy, *ibid.*, p. 320, n. 35). The sectary, Meswi al Okhbari, hesitated as to the Sunday on which Pentecost ought to be celebrated: "Meswi stated that Pentecost ought to be celebrated on a Sunday, but he did not know exactly which Sunday.... For this reason he celebrated it with the majority (of the Rabbanites)" trans. Nemoy, "Al-Qirqisani's account of the Jewish sects," *H.U.C.A.* VII (1930), p. 390. Similar hesitation is found among the Karaites of Basra (*ibid.*, p. 395). The Falashas rejected the Pentecost of 12 Siwan, thus they reckoned the 50 days from the last day of the feast; cf. Morgenstern, *V.T.*, V (1955), p. 51.

38. Cf. pp. 39-40. This period of fifty days was very carefully maintained in the calendar of *Jubilees* and of Qumran, given the capital importance that Pentecost, the festival of the renewal of the Alliance, had for them cf. above, p. 22). Compare a curious text of the Slavic version of Josephus on the Essenes: "They paid great attention to the 7th day, *the 7th week*, the 7th month and the 7th year" (Istrin and Pascal, *La prise de Jerusalem*, I, Paris, 1934, p. 143 on *B.J.* II 8,9). Cf. Rubinstein, *V.T.*, VI (1956), p. 308, n. 3. What is the exact significance of this seventh week? Is it simply the feast of Pentecost, or is there reference to other feasts of the 50th day? Cf. above, note 20, p. 154. Leaving out of account the Therapeuts, compare, on the Christian side, *Apostolic Constitutions*, VII, 36, 4: "one week, *seven weeks*, 7th month, 7th year ..." and the *Book of Adam and Eve* (cf. above, p. 57).

39. The *Sayings of Moses*, following the style of the priestly code, give as the day of arrival of the Hebrews coming out of the desert, 10/VII (Friday) (*IQ* 22, iii, 10; *DJD* I, p. 94); this date is "symmetrical" with that of Jos., 4,19 (10/I). Cf. above, note 9, p. 152.

40. Charles, *The Greek versions of the Testaments of the Twelve Patriarchs*, Oxford, 1908, p. 253 (a fragment of the MS of Mt. Athos, confirmed by the Armenian fragment of Cambridge.) Cf. Milik, "Le testament de Lévi en araméen," *R.B.*, LXII (1955), pp. 398-406. The date 1/I presumably represents the spring equinox; a very fine solar symbolism is here applied to the representative of the priesthood. Com-

Notes

pare the birth of Levi in *Jubilees* (see above, p. nn). The new priest of the *Test. of Levi* 18, is compared to the sun.

41. *Test. of Nephtali* 1,2 (a curious variant gives *the fourth day*. Might this be the—uncomprehending—translation into the day of the week?).

42. The following data are drawn from related works. *I Henoch*: only one date, a vision, 14/VII, Tuesday (I Hen., 60,1); cf. above note, 10, p. 152 *II Henoch*: the dates are transposed into another calendar (Vaillant edition, pp. 112-115 and 119); Henoch's ascension takes place on 1 Nisan. *Biblical antiquities*: ruin of Jerusalem, 17/IV, Friday (19,7); discourse of Josua, 16/III, Monday, day after the Feast of Weeks (var. 17/III) (Bibl. Ant. 23,2). *Pirqe Rabbi Eliezer*: Israel had received the commandments on *Friday*, the sixth day of the month, at the sixth hour (Friedlaender ed., p. 359).

43. According to a communication of Fr. Milik.

CHAPTER III

1. Cf. *Didaché*, 14,1; *Ep. Barnabas*, 15,9; Justin, *I Apol.*, 67,7.

2. In addition to the *Didaché*, the *Didascalia* and the *Canons of the Apostles*, mentioned below, note 5, note: *The 127 canons of the Apostles*, P.O., t.8, 685-686. See Tertullian, *De jejuniis* 2 and 14; Clement of Alexandria, *Strom.*, 7,12 (*G.C.S.*, 17, p. 54, Staehlin ed., t. III).

3. Cf. Bonsirven:, "Notre *statio* liturgique est elle empruntée au culte juif?", *R.S.R.*, XV (1925), pp. 258-266; Mohrmann, "Statio", *Vig. Chr.* VII (1953), pp. 221-245. Notice the importance of the sections of the guard or *mishmaroth* in the fragments of the 4Q liturgical calendar; and, on the other hand, *Taanith* 4,2, which forbids the men of the *ma'amad* to fast on the eve of the sabbath out of respect for the sabbath (contrast the Christian custom of fasting on Friday). For the term, *statio*, see Tertullian, *ibid.*; *Shepherd of Hermas, Simil.*, 5,1-2 (*statiōn*).

De Sacy has made a curious remark concerning a text of Makrizi: "The Arabic word used by Makrizi to indicate the feast of Pentecost signifies properly *statio*, or the place where one comes to a halt, to celebrate a solemnity, for example. This manner of speaking does not appear to me to correspond to any of the terms used by the Jews for Pentecost." De Sacy, *Chrestomathie arabe*, Paris, 1826-1827, I, p. 320, n. 37.

The Date of the Last Supper

4. Epiphanius, *De fide* 22 (*G.C.S.* 37, p. 522); *Didascalia of Addai*, 2, 2-4 (Nau ed, p. 225). Cf. *Book of Adam and Eve*, Malan ed., pp. 82-83.

5. *Didascalia*, chap. 21; *Didascalia of Addai, ibid.*; Epiphanius, *ibid.*; *Book of Adam and Eve*, ibid.; *Apostolic Constitutions*, VII 23.

6. English translation: Malan, *The Book of Adam and Eve*, London, 1882; German: Dillmann, A., *Das christliche Adambuch des Morgenaldes*, Göttingen, 1853. Cf. Migne, *Dictionnaire des Apocryphes*, I, Paris, 1856, c. 297-392.

7. Jub., 5,23; cf. above, note 4, pp. 150-151.

8. Mr. Grelot has been kind enough to point out to me that several of the above dates, if the names of the months are translated into numerals, coincide exactly with the table of conversion into days of the week. Thus, B: 15 Bermudah (or) 15/VIII (is) Friday. D: 12 Magabit (or) 12/VII (is) Sunday. E: 27 Gembot (or) 27/IX (is) Friday. It appears that an error has crept into F and G. As for C: 12 Takhas (or) 12/IV (is) Sunday (not Friday, as in the text).

9. Traces of related traditions must have been conserved—without being understood—in the chronicle of George the Chancellor. It is said, for example, that God made Adam enter paradise on Friday (Dindorf ed., t. I, p. 8). Other dates have obviously suffered through defective transmission or are of secondary origin.

10. *P.O.*, t. 18, p. 195.

11. Amiot, *Evangiles apocryphes*, Paris, 1952, p. 81.

12. *In Dan.*, IV, 23. See the textual discussion in *G.C.S.* 1 (1897) part 1, p. 242. Cf. *D.A.C.L.*, t. XII (1), 909-910.

13. Cf. Maries, "Le Messie issu de Levi chez Hippolyte de Rome," *R.S.R.* XXXIX (1951), *Melanges Lebreton* I, pp. 381-396.

14. Cf. above, note 40, pp. 156-157.

15. *De Pascha* ... ch. 19 (*C.S.E.L.* 3, 3, p. 266).

16. It is rather curious to note that the day of arrival of the cortege is also that of the death of Aaron in M.T., 1/IV (Friday).

17. Cf. the curious addition inserted in the manuscript of a fragment published by Haussleiter, and attributed by him to a *Commentary on Matthew* of Victorinus of Pettau: "feria VI annunciatus, feria I natus, feria V baptizatus, feria VI passus." *C.S.E.L.* 49 (1916), p. xxiii.

18. *Chronicon Paschale*, Dindorf ed., Bonn, 1832 I, pp. 6-7 (fragment of Peter of Alexandria); Socrates, *H.E.*, 5, 22 (*P.G.* 67, 629).

19. *The 127 canons of the Apostles, P.O.*, 8, 666; parallel text in the

158

Notes

Octateuch of Clement, bk. III, trans. Nau (*Le Canoniste contemporain* XXXVI (1913), p. 85).

20. Eusebius, *H.E.* V 24, 1.

21. *Ibid.*, 23, 1.

22. *Ibid.*, 25. For the Roman tradition, Irenaeus cites up to Sixtus the popes who observed the Pasch on a Sunday; this does not mean that the tradition goes no further back, but Irenaeus, who had learned from Polycarp, doubtless gave preference to the Asiatic tradition (*H.E.*, V 24, 14 f.)

23. *Ibid.*, 23, 3.

24. *Panarion* 10 (*G.C.S.* 25, Holl ed.; I, p. 203, 1.20). This interesting remark is the sole piece of information of any clarity given on this point by Epiphanius; subsequent notices (*Pan.* 11-12), in conjunction with the *Anakephalaeosis* of Book I (Holl ed. I, p. 166, 1. 20-25), have a confused, sometimes a contradictory, character. In the passage cited, Epiphanius likens the Essenes to the Samaritans. This is an opinion which might cause astonishment, yet it ought not be ignored, given the affinities of origin which are progressively being discovered between the sect of Qumran and the Samaritans. In addition to the similarities already noted—the Feast of Weeks celebrated on a Sunday, precepts common to *Jubilees* and the Samaritans, the Samaritan chronology in the *Apocalypse of Noah* (cf. Martin, *Henoch*, Paris, 1906, n. pp. 278-279)— notice should be taken of data drawn from the documents of Qumran: Samaritan pronunciations (*V.T.* III, pp. 310-311), similarities with the Samaritan edition (cf. Skehan, on 4Q Ex[a] in *J.B.L.* LXXIV (1955), pp. 182-187; Cross, 4Q on Num[b] in *R.B.* LXIII (1956), p. 56).

SECOND PART

CHAPTER ONE

1. Texts: Lagarde, *Didascalia Apostolorum Syriace*, Leipzig, 1854; Gibson (Margaret), *The Didascalia Apostolorum in Syriac, edited from a Mesopotamian Manuscript*, Cambridge, 1903. Translations with commentaries: Achelis - Flemming, *T.U.*, XXV, 2 Leipzig, 1904 (German). Funk, *Didascalia et Constitutiones Apostolorum*, t. I, Paderborn, 1906 (Latin). Nau, *La Didascalie*, Paris (2nd ed.) 1912 (French). Connolly, *Didascalia Apostolorum*, Oxford, 1929 (English).

2. Cf. Nau, p. xxi; Connolly, p. xc; Galtier, "La date de la Didascalie des Apôtres," *R.H.E.* XLII (1947), pp. 315-351.

The Date of the Last Supper

3. Charles, *Apocrypha* . . . I, p. 613. Galtier, *ibid.*, p. 348: "The general atmosphere in which the community appears to move . . . resembles more that of the second century than that of the end of the third."

4. Cf. the comparison of the deaconness and the Holy Spirit, the latter being of feminine gender in Semitic languages.

5. Cf. Schoeps, *Theologie und Geschichte des Juden-christentums*, Tübingen, 1949, pp. 61-63.

6. Apart from the numerous citations of "priestly" texts: Ezechiel and Numbers, see the doctrine of the Church-sanctuary which must not be defiled, the stress laid upon the priesthood of Aaron and the role of the Levites, the rules governing assemblies (Nau ed., pp. 112-115), the struggle against Judaizers who fear to lose the "Holy Spirit" by reason of ritual impurities (*ibid.*, pp. 213-220).

7. The divisions are those of the Nau edition, whose translation has been broadly followed. For the sake of convenience, the days of the week are designated by their modern names and not by their numeral, as in the Syriac where, for example, Wednesday is termed the fourth day of the week. Where the text has been summarized, square brackets have been used.

8. Cf. Connolly, p. 192, note.

9. XIX, 1; XIX, 6-7 and XX, 9; XIV, 15-16 and XX, 11-12; XIV, 17; XVIII, 1 and XIX, 6.

10. XIV, 4-9; 18-20; XVII, 7-8. Notice also the allusion in XIX, 2, to "the three-day martyrdom suffered by the Lord."

11. Cf. Holl, "Ein Bruchstück aus einem bisher unbekannten Brief des Epiphanius," in *Gesammelte Aufsätze zur Kirchengeschichte*, t. II, Tübingen, 1927, p. 211.

12. We may notice in passing the allusion to a *calendar dispute* among the Jews (XVII, 2) and the accusation levelled against those who "change the days" (XVII 6), or, literally, "clothe the days in error."

13. *De Fide*, 22; *Pan.*, 51,26; *Fragment* . . . , Holl, pp. 205-206.

14. *Pan.*, 70,10-12; cf. 75,6.

15. The betrayal by Judas is placed on Monday, the day when the paschal lamb was purchased, the tenth day of the month, in accordance with the symbolism of the letter *yod* which is the initial of the name, Jesus (*Frag.*, Holl, p. 205, 8-10; *Pan.*, 50,3; 70,12. Cf. *Didascalia*, chap. 9: XXVI, 1; chap. 26: XV,4; chap. 21: XIV,18). The Jews anticipated the Pasch out of fear of the crowd (*Frag.*, Holl, p. 205, 16-21). It is,

however, true that in the quite confused text of *Pan.*, 51,26, this is attributed to an error in calculation on the part of the Jews.

16. Holl, *ibid.*, p. 212.

17. Cf. *Pan.*, 51,26; 50, 1-2. *Frag.*, Holl, p. 206, where the *internal* chronology of the three days of the Passion contradicts the first account of the *Didascalia*.

18. *De Fide*, 22, *G.C.S.*, 37, p. 522 (Holl ed.).

19. *Ibid.*, p. 523.

20. *Frag.*, Holl, p. 206, 17-20.

21. *Frag.*, Holl, p. 206, 7-8.

22. Cf. Holl, pp. 212-213.

23. *Tractatus de fabrica mundi* 3, *C.S.E.L.* 49 (1916), p. 4 (Haussleiter ed.).

24. The Ethiopian text has here "sabbath" instead of "first day" (Sunday); but Dillmann explains that, according to the ancient custom of the Ethiopian Church, this word "sabbath" is to be translated as "Sunday" (Dillmann, *Das christliche Adambuch* . . . , n. 45, p. 139).

25. Malan ed., pp. 82-83.

CHAPTER TWO

1. Dix ed., p. 8.

2. Rahmani ed., Mainz, 1899, p. 41.

3. The III Council of Carthage, 397, regulates the Eucharistic fast, "with the exception of the single anniversary day when the Lord's Supper is celebrated"; chap. 29, Mansi, *Council. ampl. collectio*, t. III, col. 885.—Cf. Augustine, Ep. LIV (118), *Ad Januarium*, c. 7, *P.L.*, 33, 204.

4. Cf. *Vig. Christ.*, VIII (1954), p. 100. The date is discussed.

5. *Peregrinatio ad loca sancta*, 34, Petre ed., pp. 228-230.

6. *Ibid.*, 33, p. 224.

7. Fr. Mercier, an Armenian specialist, kindly informs me that the Armenian liturgy—the lectionary of which is very closely allied to that of Jerusalem—also places the office of Tuesday evening on the Mt. of Olives. It is even possible to pick out in this office certain dominant themes which are of interest to our purpose: the messianic banquet (Prov., 9,1-11: the banquet of Wisdom) or the betrayal by Judas—but it is question more of the moral betrayal (to the chief priests) than of the actual betrayal in the garden (see above, pp. 89-90).

161

The Date of the Last Supper

8. *Adv. Haer.*, II, 22,3 (Harvey ed., t. I, p. 329).

9. *P.G.*, 92, 80. Dindorf ed., I, pp. 13-14.

10. See below (p. 95), the exposition of the difficulties for exegesis arising out of the date of the death of Jesus.

11. *P.G.*, 92, 81. Dindorf, I, p. 14.

12. *G.C.S.*, 17, p. 216 (Stählin ed., t. III).

13. "Christ, our Pasch, is sacrificed": I Cor., 5,7.—Cf. Apoc., 5, 6-13.
—Justin, *Dialogue*, 111,3. *Gospel of Peter*, II, 5b. We have already seen the evidence of Apollinaris. Hippolytus also states that Jesus did not eat the Pasch, but that he suffered (fragment of the *Chronicon Paschale*, *G.C.S.* 1, part 2, p. 270, Bonwetsch ed.). "The precise disposition of the days" concerns also, according to the continuation of Clement's text, the fixed dates of Friday and Sunday: "The resurrection also bears witness (to this exactitude): for he rose the third day. which was the first of the weeks of harvest, when the law prescribed that the priest should offer the sheaf of corn."

14. Eusebius, *H.E.*, IV 26,4; VI 13,9.

15. The date may be deduced from the reference to the proconsulate of Servilius Paulus at Laodicaea, between 164 and 168 (Eusebius, *H.E.* IV 26,3).

16. *I Apol.* 66,3; *Dial.* 41,3.

17. (*Dial.*, 111,3). *En hēmera tou pascha sunelabete auton kai omoiōs en tō pascha estaurōsate gegraptai.*

18. *Ep. can.*, chap. 15 (*P.G.*, 18, 508b).

19. *Didascalia of Addai*, 2,3 (Nau ed., p. 225).

20. The fact is so obvious that an exegete such as Fr. Lagrange could write: "The Christian tradition considered Wednesday as the beginning of the passion" (*Evangile selon saint Marc*, Paris, 1942, p. 365, n. 1).

THIRD PART

CHAPTER ONE

1. The question has given rise to a vast literature. It is not possible to give an exhaustive list here. The following may be consulted: Str.-Bill. II, Exkurs, pp. 812-853, "Der Todestag Jesu." Lagrange, *Evangile selon saint Marc*, 1942, pp. 354-363. G. Ogg, *The Chronology of the Public Ministry of Jesus*, Cambridge, 1940, pp. 205-242. Among the most

Notes

recent publications, the following may be noted. In *J.Q.R.*, XLII (1951-1952) the opposed theses of Heawood and Zeitlin (pp. 37-50) and of Torrey and Zeitlin (pp. 237-260); the English translation of the work of J. Jeremias, *The Eucharistic Words of Jesus*, Oxford, 1955.

2. Cf., for example, Theodore Reinach on the difficulties arising out of the accounts of the passion: "The incoherence and the contradictions of these accounts prove that they are devoid, in their details, of all historical foundation." *R.E.J.*, XXXV (1897), p. 16, n. 1.

3. The expression has always been the source of difficulty, particularly in a system where this first day of Azymes had to fall *two days before* the Pasch, that is, 13 Nisan! However, the expression may be accurately applied to the eve of the Pasch, for already in the morning of this day the use of leavened bread was forbidden. See Str.-Bill., *ibid.*, pp. 813-815, where rabbinical parallels are given.

4. It is scarcely likely that the priests would have permitted the slaughter of lambs in the Temple on any other than the official day. The question to be answered is whether, among the Jewish groups who celebrated the Pasch on a fixed day, the slaughter of the lamb was preserved. Since the discovery at Qumran of bones belonging to sacred banquets and carefully preserved in pots (*R.B.*, LXIII (1956), pp. 74, 549-550), it seems very likely that the lamb was immolated at Qumran, the community itself fulfilling the role of the sanctuary. But when we leave the Temple of Jerusalem and the community of Qumran, considered as a sanctuary, the problem becomes much more difficult to solve. For Elephantine, cf. Grelot, "Le Papyrus pascal et le problème du Pentateuque," *V.T.*, V (1955), pp. 160-262. For examples of immolation of the paschal lamb outside Palestine, see the references given by Pedersen, *Israel. Its Life and its Culture*, II, London - Copenhagen, 1940, pp. 413-414, and the corresponding notes, pp. 705, 707. See also *P.G.*, 1, 870 (*Variorum notae*): the Armenians betray Judaizing tendencies because they immolate the paschal lamb. In spite of these examples, it may be questioned whether, in many cases, a ritual of unleavened bread was not sufficient for the celebration of the Pasch. This solution appears the most likely for the Supper of Jesus.

5. Cf. Jn., 2,6-10 (the water of Jewish purification is replaced by the excellent wine provided by Jesus). Jn., 4,11-14 (the water of the well at which Jacob and his children had drunk is replaced by the water springing up, given by Jesus), etc.

6. Cf. Jn., 2,13-22 (at the approach of the Pasch *of the Jews*, Jesus expels the beasts of sacrifice from the Temple; it is he who will

build the new Temple). Jn., 6,4 f. (at the approach of the Pasch, *the festival of the Jews,* Jesus multiplies the loaves, symbol of the Eucharist). Jn., 7,2.37-39 (on the last day of the Feast of Tabernacles, *the feast of the Jews,* Jesus issues his invitation to drink from the springing stream of the Spirit).

7. The fact that the fourth Gospel adopts the point of view of the official feasts should not be allowed to obscure the "sensibility" of the same Gospel for the days of the week (Mgr. Weber has stressed this point in the *Bulletin ecclésiastique du diocèse de Strasbourg,* LXXIV (1955), p. 542). The days have been scrupulously noted in several passages of the fourth Gospel; the author doubtless had his own carefully considered reasons for this, and these reasons ought not to be left out of account. After the "running in" which we have received from the priestly documents, *Jubilees,* and the *Book of Adam and Eve,* this should not surprise us. The details of Jn., 1,29 – 2,1, in this regard, have already given rise to very many interpretations. And, independently of all question of calendars, several critics had already suggested that the wedding of Cana must have fallen on a *Wednesday,* since, in ancient times, the weddings of Jewish girls were customarily fixed on that day (cf. Str.-Bill. II 398; Bultmann, *Das Evangelium des Johannes,* 12th ed., 1952, p. 79, n. 3). See also above, note 23, pp. 149-150, on the customs of the ancient *hasidim.* Accordingly, this meal at Cana, which, in the intention of the author, foretells the Last Supper, would prefigure it also by the symbolism of the day itself, brought into prominence by the evangelist. In this case, the *tē tritē hēmera* (Jn., 2,1) can be interpreted in the absolute sense as the third day (of the week), that is, Tuesday, towards the evening of which, at the beginning of the night of Wednesday, the wedding meal was held. But it may equally well be interpreted as the third day after the "next day" of 1,43, in which case the latter is a *Sunday.* It is precisely on this day after the sabbath that Jesus sets out for Galilee (the distance may easily be covered in three days' march). Taking note of the *prōton* of 1,41, the previous day is the sabbath; it is noted that the disciples remained with Jesus that day. Two days before, when John the Baptist makes his great proclamation of the lamb who takes away the sins of the world, is a *Friday.*

Once again the complementary characteristics of the fourth Gospel become apparent: rooted in the world of Palestine, it is, nevertheless, adapted to the Hellenistic world.

8. Cf. above, p. 62.

9. Cf. above, p. 85.

Notes

10. The parallel text of Luke—which does not mention the anointing at Bethany (cf. Lk., 7,36 f.)—gives no precise information on dates: "The feast of Unleavened Bread *was approaching*, that which is called the Pasch" (Lk., 22,1). This vague expression, which recalls the formulas of St. John, perhaps betrays a certain embarrassment on the part of the author. In its present redaction, this text *could* refer to the legal feast.

11. Jesus would arrive at Bethany on a sabbath day. A difficulty might be seen here; but it could be resolved in various ways: the sabbath ended at sunset; Jesus could have come from a neighbouring locality; the term "come" should not be pressed too closely.

12. The equivalent phrases of Josephus *meta duo etē B.J.*, I, 13,1) (or) *deuterō etei* (A.J., XIV, 13,3) and *meta tessarakonta hēmeras* (B.J., L, 16,2) (or) *eis tessarakostēn hēmeran* (A.J., XIV, 15,4) are hardly favorable to the longer period. But there is an example in George The Chancellor, *Chronicle* (Dindorf ed., t. I, p. 8) in which the period between the 40th and the 44th day is expressed by *meta treis hēmeras*.

In the third account of the *Didascalia*, later than the first according to internal criticism, the meal of Simon the Leper is placed on a Monday (Sunday evening?), but, it seems, this is in order to be able to apply the symbolism of the choice of the paschal lamb on Monday (10 Nisan). Nau ed., pp. 172-173. See also Nau's note on this passage.

13. Matt., 21,18-22, combines in a single day the two phases of the account.

Fr. Daniélou, in *Maison-Dieu*, 46, pp. 119-130, suggests that Jesus' entry into Jerusalem on Palm Sunday should be placed in September. The hypothesis is a difficult one, for, in John, the entry of the Palms takes place the day after the anointing—which was six days before the Pasch (Jn., 12,1.12); and also because, in Mark, the present account stresses that "it was not the season for figs" (Mk., 11.13), an indication that the editor had no memory of an entry with palms in the fall. We do not know at what time the liturgical lessons of the ancient priestly calendar began.

14. Juda's interview with the priests—the moral betrayal—would take place on Sunday or Monday (Mk., 14,10 and parall.; cf. Jn., 13,2).

The Date of the Last Supper

CHAPTER TWO

1. The full Sanhedrin was composed of 71 members (*Sanh.*, 1,6); but 23 members were sufficient to judge a capital case (*Sanh.*, 4,1). Mark's expressions would indicate a plenary session.

2. Herod did not permit Jesus to leave until he had fruitlessly attempted to make him speak.

3. *Apostolic Tradition*, Dix ed., pp. 62-63. Cf. *Canons* of Hippolytus (*ibid.*) and the *Testament of O. L. Jesus Christ* (Rahmani ed., pp. 144-145).

4. In the perspective of the Synoptics a very clear and eventful period elapses between the crucifixion and the darkness at the 6th hour.

5. *Frag.*, Holl, p. 206, 1. 22-30.

6. Origen—in the texts which we have been able to discover—is primarily sensible to the symbolism of the 6th hour, darkness at mid-day. There is no discussion of the exact hour of the crucifixion (*Comm. on Cant.*, II, *G.C.S.* 33,140); but the 6th hour is suggested in *Math. comm. ser.* 134, *G.C.S.*, 38, 277). It is curious to see Jerome invert the palaeographical argument to the detriment of the 3rd hour (*Brev. in Ps.* LXXVII, *P.L.* 26, 1046); in any event, this is proof that the problem was recognized.

7. Greek chain: *P.G.*, 22,1009. Severus of Antioch: *P.O.* 14, 270-272.

8. "The evangelist, John, says in his Gospel: . . . *It was the eve of the Pasch; it was about the 3rd hour,* as appears in the exact copies and in the copy written by the hand of the evangelist himself which, by the grace of God, is preserved up to the present day in the most holy church of Ephesus and is there venerated by the faithful" (*Chronicon paschale,* Dindorf ed., I, pp. 10-11, Bonn, 1892).

9. Surprise has often been expressed because Jesus died after only three hours on the cross. In the suggested chronology, he dies after 2½ days of suffering and after six hours on the cross.

10. Marmardji ed., established Arabic text, translated into French (Beyreuth, 1935), pp. 463 f.

11. This is the exegesis of Fr. Benoit in *Angelicum,* XX (1943), "Jesus devant le Sanhedrin," pp. 158-160.

12. Mark (like Luke) does not name this high priest (Mk., 14,53). The determination, "Caiphas," in Matt., 26,57, is doubtless due to a Greek editor of the text.

13. A "legal" trial certainly did not take place in the house of the high priest (cf. Str.-Bill. I, pp. 997-1001). "As soon as it was day,

the ancients of the people, and the chief priests and scribes came together, and they *had him led* (*apēgagon*) into their council" Lk., 22,66). This would indicate a change of location, even if *sunedrion* signifies here the assembly and not the place where it met.—Cf. Benoit, *ibid.*, p. 165.

14. As on the day when Pilate wished to have brought into Jerusalem the Roman insignia and the images of the emperors (Josephus, *A.J.*, XVIII, 3,1; *B.J.*, II, 9,2-3). A decision of Pilate could have no value in the eyes of the Jews.

15. No early Christian text accuses the judgment of the leaders of the nation of illegality. Yet it would have been a simple polemical argument.

16. *Christus,* 11 (July, 1956), p. 418.

17. Appeal has been made to *Sanh.*, 11,4, which speaks of exemplary punishments administered during restivals in order to impress the people; but this text is incapable of resolving either the contradiction in the Gospels or the juridical difficulty, for the condemned person had to be judged previously and kept in custody for the feast.

18. The mockery: "Christ, prophesy" (Matt., 26,68 and parall.), is normally placed after Jesus' declaration before the high priest; this is the order in Mk./Matt. In Luke, however, where only one session of the Sanhedrin is noted, after which Jesus is immediately brought before Pilate, the mockery has to be situated before the session (Lk., 22,63-65).

19. Jesus doubtless spent the night of Wednesday to Thursday in prison; the same is true of the night of Thursday to Friday, but this time under the guard of Pilate's jailers. A reference to Jesus' imprisonment might be seen in the words of Peter, reported *after the event*: "I am ready to go with you *to prison* and to death" (Lk., 22,33).

20. See Str.-Bill., II (1924), pp. 838-839. I owe this reference to Fr. Vogt who drew my attention to this text.

21. It will be seen that the suggested chronology, far from sacrificing the historicity of Jn., 18,28 (cf. the hasty interpretation of Burkill, "The Last Supper," *Numen,* III (1956), p. 177, n. 35), gives full value to the different indications of time given by John's Gospel: *"Before* the feast of the Pasch"* (Tuesday evening); they refused to defile themselves "so that they might eat the Pasch" (Thursday morning); "it was the *eve* of the Pasch" (Friday morning).

22. The (*sunēgmenōn autōn*) of Matt., 27,17 seems to be the recollection of an assembly convened by Pilate. The episode of Judas' remorse and of his interview with the chief priests is inserted into the

context of the appearance before Pilate (27,3-10). The perturbing experience of Pilate's wife during the night becomes easy to understand if she was disturbed about the prisoner who had been handed over to her husband the day before (27,19).

23. Cf. the skepticism of Juster, *Les Juifs dans l'Empire romain,* Paris, 1914, II, pp. 127-149. See bibliography in O. Cullmann, *Der Staat im Neuen Testament,* Tübingen, 1956, p. 28, n. 1 (French trans.: *Dieu et César,* p. 44 and n. 16).

24. *Jesus,* 2nd ed., 1950, p. 412. In the same work, Mr. Goguel pointed out that, in the Johannine tradition, there existed "a certain void" between the entry of Jesus into Jerusalem and the Last Supper (p. 186); he even suggested that the Supper might have taken place prior to the eve of Jesus' death (p. 187, n. 5).

25. Cf. Josephus, *B.J.,* II 8,1; *A.J.,* XX, 9,1. The Romans doubtless closed their eyes to purely internal matters or to those arising exclusively from Jewish law (cf. the stoning of Stephen). It is certainly necessary to distinguish between the theoretical letter of the law and actual application. Cf. also Burkill, "The competence of the Sanhedrin," *Vig. Christ.* X (1956), pp. 80-86.

26. See O. Cullmann's analyses of the zealot movement around Jesus and of the Roman trial (*ibid.,* pp. 5-35; *Dieu et César,* pp. 11-53).

27. The episode of Pilate's wife suggests that attempts were made to save Jesus.

28. As regards the question of the divergence existing between Mk./Matt. and Jn. on the time of the crowning with thorns, the likelihood is on the side of John who places the crowning scene during the dialogue between Pilate and the Jews. On the contrary, the scourging must have taken place, in accordance with the normal practice, before the punishment (*phragellōsas*) Mk., 15,15/Matt., 27,26, which does not exclude the "chastisement" administered by Pilate (Jn., 19,1; Lk., 23, 16.22).

CONCLUSION

1. Ecclus., 33,7-9. Cf. text of *Bible de Jérusalem.*

2. If the already established days had been other than they were, it would, doubtless, have been possible to give prominence to Thursday, the day of the verdict; to Saturday, when Jesus was in the tomb; in fact, the coincidences were less remarkable. In places where the day was

Notes

considered to begin at sunrise there would have been a tendency to forget Tuesday evening. It may be noted that the Friday of the crucifixion replaced the Friday of the Feast of Expiations (10/VII).

3. This symbolism is certainly stressed in John (20,1.19); the final apparition, which opens the time of the Church, takes place "eight days later" (20,26). Cf. in the *Slavic Henoch,* the prominence given to Sunday, the first and the eighth day (Vaillant ed., pp. 102-105). Also, the *Epistle of Barnabas,* 15,8-9, and Justin, *Dial.,* 41,4; 138,1; I *Apol.,* 67,7.

APPENDIX II

1. On the planetary week in Hebrew literature, Mr. Vajda has been kind enough to point out to me the article of S. Gandz in *Proceedings of the American Academy for Jewish Research,* XVIII (1948-1949), pp. 213-254.

2. Since each year this Wednesday is 1¼ days behind the solar year. This text *seems* to indicate that there were two ways of calculating the equinox, one on a Sunday (the common usage), the other on a Wednesday (a minority usage, the one which interests us here). The calculation presupposes that the week in which the spring equinox falls is known; if it is not, then it is necessary, from the seventh year of the cycle, to add from one to four weeks in order to find the *tequfah.* We remain ignorant of the manner in which such a calculation intercalated 35 days or 5 weeks in 28 years. A tradition of placing the equinox on Sunday, the first day of creation, will be found among Christian writers (App. III, note 2, p. 170).

3. By adding the four days of Tishri to the preceding six months, of which three have 29 days (Elul, Tamuz, Iyar) and three have 30 days (Abh, Siwan, Nisan).

In the *Pirke,* the sun and moon were created on 28 Elul (Frielaender ed., p. 52); this tradition is opposed to the reckoning from Nisan (*ibid.,* p. 35).

4. Cf. the lively discussion of *Rosh Hashanah* 11a between R. Jehosua and R. Eliezer. For Philo the world had been created in springtime (*Spec. leg.,* II 151-152); so also for ancient Christian writers (cf. App. III, pp. 138-139).

5. Cf. *D.A.C.L., ibid.,* c. 1532-1534, particularly c. 1533, n. 3. There is little to be found from this point of view in Krush, *Studien zur*

169

The Date of the Last Supper

christlichmitteralt. Chronology. Der 84-jährige Ostercyclus und seine Quellen, Leipzig, 1880.

APPENDIX III

1. This statement must be off-set by the indication in the opposite sense given in Qirqisani's description of the Jewish sects: Nemoy's trans. in *H.U.C.A.,* VII (1930), p. 363: "the Magarya determine the beginning of the month by the appearance of the new moon." This contradiction indicates, perhaps, that there took place a transfer from the full moon to the new moon at the beginning of the month (cf. p. 140), but later writers, such as Al-Biruni and Qirqisani, were unable to recognize the varying dates of the documents which they had assembled.

2. Here might be seen an unconscious survival of the memory of the Wednesday Pasch. But Christian tradition was far from being uniform. Other currents were to be found: a) the day of Easter, celebrated on Sunday, was placed in relation with the first day of creation, as being the new creation and thus the anniversary of the birth of the world (cf. *P.G.,* 5, 1369; *Book of Adam and Eve,* p. 82; Eusebius, *P.G.,* 24, 697); this Sunday of creation was situated at the spring equinox, for on the first day God had divided light and darkness into equal parts (*P.G.,* 5, 1368; *P.L.,* 13, 1108); b) Christ's death, according to the most ancient date known to us, that of Hippolytus (paschal table and *In Dan.* IV, 23,3), fell on Friday, March 25, thus in coincidence with the spring equinox. Thus Christ's death redeemed the world on the anniversary of the very day of creation; hence also the date of the Annunciation (March 25), since Christ could only have passed a perfect number of years on earth (cf. Duchesne, *Origines du culte chrétien,* Paris, 1902, pp. 262-263).

All these various forms of symbolism were unfavorable to the preservation of the memory of a Wednesday Pasch.

3. Morgenstern considers that the Pasch was originally celebrated at the new moon of the month of Abib (interpretation of *hodesh* in Ex., 34,18; Deut., 16,1); see *H.U.C.A.,* X (1935), "Supplementary Studies in the Calendars of ancient Israel," pp. 5-7.

It might be asked whether, at some time in the history of Israel, there did not take place a transfer of the full moon from the first day of the month; but, whatever may have been the system of numbering, the beginning of the calculation would always have been assigned to the full moon of the fourth day of creation.

4. The identification is rendered all the more likely when it is recalled that, on the witness of the Karaite, Qirqisani, the "Sadducees" had 30 days in all their months (*H.U.C.A.*, VII (1930), p. 363).

5. A recent document of 4Q illumines this problem. See the communication, revised and completed, of Milik, *Supplement to V.T.*, IV, p. 25. The lunar calendar could be synchronized with the calendar of 364 days at the end of 3 years by the addition of a month of 30 days to the lunar calendar: 364 X 3 (is) 354 X 3 plus 30. Might it not be possible to relate this intercalation of a month of 30 days to the text of Al-Biruni cited above, p. 46.

6. The document of 4Q, already cited, proves precisely the contrary; (see foregoing note).

7. Two Hebrew fragments of *Ecclus.* have been found in cave 2 (*R.B.*, LXIII (1956), p. 54). This writing, however, cannot rival *Jubilees*, the manuscripts of which are much more numerous.

CONCORDANCE TABLE

	MATTHEW	MARK	LUKE	JOHN
TUESDAY. **PREPARATION OF THE PASCH** (*ancient calendar*)	26, 17-19. The first day of Azymes...	14, 12-16. The first day of Azymes, when they sacrificed the Pasch...	22, 7-13. The day of Azymes came when the Pasch was to be sacrificed.	13, 1-2. Before the feast of the Pasch (*official calendar*)... Jesus loved his own to the end, and during the meal...
	they prepared the Pasch.	they prepared the Pasch.	...they prepared the Pasch.	
Evening (beginning of Wednesday) **SUPPER**	20. In the evening he went to table with his disciples...	17-18. In the evening whilst they were at table...	14-15. When the hour came, he sat down at table..."With desire I have desired to eat this Pasch with you, before I suffer."	18, 2-11.
NIGHT. ARREST	47-56.	43-52.	47-53.	
JESUS LED BEFORE ANNAS.	57a. They led Jesus to the high priest. 58. Peter followed.	53a. They led Jesus to the high priest. 54. Peter followed.	54a. They led him to the house of the high priest. 54b. Peter followed.	12-13. They bound him and led him *first* to *Annas*. 15. Peter followed.
INTERROGATION				16-18. First denial. 19-23. *Interrogation* by high priest.
PETER'S DENIALS.	69-75. (Triple denial and crowing of cock.)	67-72. (Triple denial and crowing of cock.)	55-60. (Triple denial and crowing of cock.)	25-27. (Last denial and crowing of cock.)
JESUS LED BEFORE CAIPHAS.	57a. Cuiphas...		61-62. Turning round, the Lord looked at Peter.	24. Annas sent him bound to the high priest, Caiphas.

WEDNESDAY.			
MEETING of SANHEDRIN.	57b. Scribes a n d ancients assembled.	53b. All the chief priests the ancients a n d t h e scribes assembled.	66a. As soon as it was *day,* the council of the ancients of the people, the chief priests and the scribes assembled.
JESUS APPEARED before the SANHEDRIN.			66b. And they had him brought before their Sanhedrin.
TRIAL SESSION.	59-61. They sought false witnesses and found none. Yet many came f o r - ward.	55-60. They sought witnesses and found none; y e t m a n y bore false witness and they did not agree. A n d some stood up...	
APPEARANCE of WITNESSES.	*Finally* t w o came forward...		
ADJURATION of HIGH PRIEST.	62-66. "A r t thou the Christ? What more need have we of witnesses?"	61-64. AS MATT.	67-71. "If thou art the Christ, tell us"... "What more need have we of witnesses?"
OUTRAGES to the FALSE MESSIAH.	67-68. "Messiah, prophesy..."	65. "Prophesy."	Cf. 63-65.
Night in prison — *at house of Caiphas ?*			

CONCORDANCE TABLE

THURSDAY	MATTHEW	MARK	LUKE	JOHN
VERDICT SESSION.	27, 1. When *morning was come*, all the chief priests and the ancients of the people held a council against Jesus so as to *put him to death*..	15, 1a. *In the morning*, when the chief priests and all the Sanhedrin had deliberated with the ancients and the scribes..		
JESUS LED BEFORE PILATE.	2. Having bound him, they led him away and handed him over to the Governor, Pilate.	1b. AS MATT.	23, 1. Their whole assembly rose up and they led him to Pilate.	18, 28. Thus they led Jesus from the house of Caiphas to the pretorium. It was the *morning*. But they did not enter **the pretorium** that they might not be **defiled** and that they *might eat the Pasch.*
				29a. Pilate came out and appeared before them.
ACCUSATION BEFORE THE GOVERNOR.	12. As he was accused by the chief priests and the ancients.	3.The chief priests brought many accusations against him.	2. Then they began to accuse him: this man stirs up our nation..	29b-32. "What charge do you bring against this man?"...
PILATE QUESTIONS JESUS.	11. "Art thou the King of the Jews?"	2. AS MATT.	3. "Art thou t h e king of t h e Jews?"... I find no cause in this man.	33-38. "Art thou the king of the Jews?"... I find no cause in him...
SENT TO HEROD.			6-12. Herod questioned him with many words. The chief priests and the scribes accused him violently. Herod mocks him.	
DISPERSION OF CHIEF PRIESTS.	Cf. 3-10. Remorse of Judas.			
CAMPAIGN AMONG THE PEOPLE.	20. They had persuaded the crowd..	11. The chief priests had stirred up the crowd.		
Night in prison	19. (Pilate's wife			

GREAT ASSEMBLY BEFORE THE PRETORIUM.	17a. Pilate *brought* them *together*.	8. The crowd having come up, they began to complain...	13. Pilate *summoned* the chief priests and the leaders of the people...	
SECOND SESSION BEFORE PILATE.	17b. (Jesus or Barabbas?)	9. "Shall I release to you the king of the Jews?"	18-19. "Release to us Barabbas!"	39-40. They called for Barabbas.
CROWNING WITH THORNS.	27-31.	16-20.	Cf. 16. 22.	19, 1-5. Pilate had him scourged. Crowning with thorns.
HESITATIONS OF THE GOVERNOR.	21-25. Taking the word, the governor said to them...	12-14. Once again Pilate spoke...	20. Once again Pilate spoke to them... 22. A third time he said to them.	4. Once again Pilate came out. 12. Pilate sought to free him.
CONDEMNATION AND SCOURGING.	26.	15.	24-25.	14-16. It w a s the *eve of the* Pasch, towards the 6th (?) hour.
CLIMB TO CALVARY.	32-34.	21-22.	26-32.	17.
CRUCIFIXION.	35-44.	25-32. It was the *3rd hour.*	33-43.	18-29.
DARKNESS.	45. From the 6th hour to the 9th hour	33. From the 6th to the 9th hour.	44. From the 6th to the 9th hour.	
DEATH OF JESUS.	46-50. Ninth hour.	34-37. 9th hour. 46.	46.	30.

JUBILEES CALENDAR

TRIMESTRAL TABLE

I.	IV.	VII.	X.
1	8	15	22	29
2	9	16	23	30
3	10	17	24	
4	11	18	25	
5	12	19	26	
6	13	20	27	
7	14	21	28	

II.	V.	VIII.	XI.
	6	13	20	27
	7	14	21	28
1	8	15	22	29
2	9	16	23	30
3	10	17	24	
4	11	18	25	
5	12	19	26	

III.	VI.	IX.	XII.	
	4	11	18	25 : Wednes.
	5	12	19	26 : Thurs.
	6	13	20	27 : Friday
	7	14	21	28 : Saturday
1	8	15	22	29 : Sunday
2	9	16	23	30 : Monday
3	10	17	24	31 : Tuesday

The months are in Roman numerals. The days of the week were always indicated by their numeral: 1st day (Sunday), 2nd day (Monday), etc.